SEASON

OF

SATURDAYS

A HISTORY OF
COLLEGE FOOTBALL
IN 14 GAMES

MICHAEL WEINREB

SCRIBNER

NEW YORK   LONDON   TORONTO   SYDNEY   NEW DELHI

SCRIBNER
A Division of Simon & Schuster, Inc.
1230 Avenue of the Americas
New York, NY 10020

First Scribner hardcover edition August 2014

For information about special discounts for bulk purchases, please contact Simon
& Schuster Special Sales at 1-866-506-1949 or business@simonandschuster.com.

The Simon & Schuster Speakers Bureau can bring authors to your live event. For
more information or to book an event, contact the Simon & Schuster Speakers
Bureau at 1-866-248-3049 or visit our website at www.simonspeakers.com.

Interior design by Jill Putorti
Jacket design by Gregg Kulick
Jacket photographs: Ohio State Coach Woody Hayes © Tony Tomsic/Contributor/
Sports Illustrated/Getty Images; University of Notre Dame Football Memorabilia ©
Todd Rosenberg/Contributor/*Sports Illustrated*/Getty Images; University of Miami—
Vinny Testaverde © Carl Skalak/Contributor/*Sports Illustrated*/Getty Images;
Michigan State University Spartans—Bubba Smith © Collegiate Images/Contributor/
Getty Images; University of Alabama Coach Paul "Bear" Bryant © Heinz Kluetmeier/
Contributor/*Sports Illustrated*/Getty Images; Washington State v. Oregon © Steve
Dykes/Stringer/Getty Images Sport/Getty Images

Manufactured in the United States of America

10 9 8 7 6 5 4 3 2 1

Library of Congress Cataloging-in-Publication Data is available.

ISBN 978-1-4516-2781-7
ISBN 978-1-4516-2784-8 (ebook)

Portions of this work appeared, in different form, on Grantland.com.

To State College, Pennsylvania
My hometown

CONTENTS

SEASON
OF
SATURDAYS

A PREFACE

So maybe you already understand:

Maybe you are nine years old, and your father takes you to a college football game. You reside in the vicinity of a sprawling state university; the stadium looms on the outskirts of campus, a clunky leviathan of exposed steel beams and concrete pillars, surrounded by freshman dormitories and parking lots and acres of muddy agricultural pastureland. The roads are narrow, the traffic is suffocating, and the tailgates go on for miles, tethered to recreational vehicles and trailers and pickup trucks. Everything is so huge; even the air seems weighed down with smells, charred meat, and churned-up dirt and manure of varied origins. You pass into the stadium through Gate E and the ramps are too narrow and the people too thick (both individually, because this is rural

America, and collectively, because the game is a sellout), and you stand there and wait for the arteries to clear (both figuratively and literally), and every so often, you hear adults buzzed on cheap pilsner bellow like corralled cattle to pass the time.

Maybe all of this rings familiar to you. Maybe this was your childhood, too.

For me, it goes back to 1982, when prime-time college football was not yet a regular thing, packaged by cable television into a commodified national experience. For me, it was Nebraska at Penn State, a matchup of top-ten programs in front of eighty-five thousand people, the first game in the history of this particular stadium that required lights (the lights were portable, mounted on trucks, and given to frequent short-circuiting). The home team led 14–0 early, and then they trailed 24–21 late in the fourth quarter, and I could not see most of what happened after that, because I was too small and everyone around me was standing and I was engulfed in a thicket of down jackets and cigar smoke and pocket radio antennas and the voice of a guy named Steve was critiquing the play-calling.

At that point, my memory blends with the television replays, and because I tend to recall my childhood in snapshots, I have retained this photographic image of the stadium clock showing one minute, eighteen seconds remaining in the fourth quarter. And in conjunction with this image, I recall trying to count seventy-eight seconds in my head during the commercial time-out as Penn State awaited the kickoff for the last drive of the game, as if I might somehow be able to slow the progress of time by deconstructing it inside my own head. (It's almost as if I was already nostalgic for what was about to happen.)

There was a throw to the sideline, to a Penn State tight end who was clearly out of bounds but was ruled in bounds, for reasons that either defy explanation or raise suspicion, depending upon one's perspective; there was a throw to the end zone, to a klutzy tight end whose nickname was actually Stonehands, who cradled the pass in his arms and toppled to the ground for the game-winning touchdown. And I remember the quake and the aftershocks inside that stadium, and I remember the bacchanalia outside, and I remember listening to the radio broadcast in the car, and I remember watching the highlights on the news and on television the next morning, and I remember thinking that I would never, in the course of my life, see anything bigger than that again.

It's a difficult thing to quantify: the elation, the connection, the sense of belonging that college football provides. But then, maybe you don't need me to tell you. Maybe you already understand.

Or maybe you don't understand at all:

Maybe you attended a liberal arts college in New England, or maybe you grew up in a city where the athletes were professionals (New York, say, or Boston, or Chicago, or London). Maybe the very idea of college football resided at the far edge of your consciousness, a rural preoccupation like Garth Brooks and Peanut Buster Parfaits and moonshine, the province of southerners and state-school graduates and scrubbed fraternity boys in hooded sweatshirts. Maybe the thought of a university's morale being tied to its football team strikes you as a fundamental failing of American society. Maybe you hear stories about corrupt recruiting and grade-fixing, and maybe you cannot understand how a sport with a long history of exploitation and brutality and scandal can still be considered a vital (and often defining) aspect of student life. Maybe you see it as a potentially crippling frivolity, or as a populist indulgence, and maybe the threat of football encroaching on the nation's educational system makes you wonder how someone could possibly write an entire book extolling its cultural virtues.

And the thing is, I would like to tell you that you're wrong, but I also know that you're not *entirely* wrong.

I am writing this in the fall of 2013, as college football reaches a turning point: In 2014, a four-team playoff will commence, the most tacit acknowledgment to date from the NCAA that the sport is no longer an amateur pursuit. There are lawsuits pending as to whether college athletes will be able to trade on their name and likeness, and there are debates over whether they should be paid a stipend or whether the sport should be opened up to the free market. All of this is happening at the same time as we ponder legitimate questions about whether the sport of football is too violent to exist at all.

After the Penn State child sex abuse scandal broke in 2011, I wrote some words that got circulated online and I somehow briefly became a de facto spokesman for my hometown; in the process, I had people asking me multiple versions of the same question: *Why does college football exist?* It came from graduates of East Coast private schools that did not field football teams, from hard-core academics who saw college football as anathematic to their own purposes, from writers in Brooklyn who viewed college football as a simple-minded "southern thing."

So this book is an attempt to convey why college football means so much to me, and maybe to you, if you grew up in a place like my hometown of State College, Pennsylvania, or if you graduated from a school like Michigan or Ohio State or Alabama or Texas, or if you are one of the roughly 50 million Americans who attended a college football game last season. It is a cultural history and a personal history and it is an exercise in nostalgia; it is a lamentation of the sport's enduring stubbornness and a celebration of its enduring innocence. It is a sentimental defense of college football from an obsessive fan who still lulls himself to sleep by thinking about the end of that '82 Nebraska game, and it is an attempt to detail how college football's long history of scandal and politicization and bureaucratic infighting have led us to this point. It is an exploration of the varied meanings that college football holds for so many otherwise rational Americans, and it is an exploration of the ways that college football, in arousing such passion (and such unabashed hatred), has come to reflect our national (and regional) identity. No other nation in the world can even fathom the notion of attaching a prominent moneymaking athletic operation to a university; the fact that college football has existed for nearly 150 years, and the fact that it remains one of the most popular sports in America, must say *something* about who we are.

I grew up with college football in my blood. I am not so blinded as to fail to recognize its inherent hypocrisies, and yet I still enjoy it more purely and completely than I enjoy almost anything else in my life. I don't want it to die. I don't want it to fall victim to corruption and violence; I don't want it to wither in a courtroom due to the failures of bureaucrats. I want it to find a rational path beyond this point of crisis. I want people to understand.

What follows is my attempt to explain.

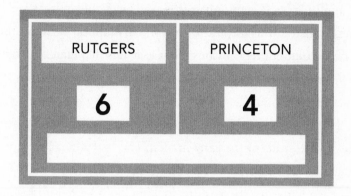

RUTGERS	PRINCETON
6	4

November 6, 1869

You Men Will Come to No Christian End!

Discussion Topics: Yale • Harvard • Walter Camp • Fried Beef Hearts • Charles Eliot • The Flying Wedge • Teddy Roosevelt • Death • The Forward Pass • Nick Saban

I.

A young man at the turn of the twentieth century, the son of Irish immigrants, wins a scholarship to Exeter, an exclusive New England prep school. He enrolls at the advanced age of twenty-three (he had been earning his own living up to then) and he pays his room and his board by working maintenance and waiting tables. He becomes an immensely popular figure on campus; he is named captain of the football team. At twenty-seven, he is wooed by multiple Ivy League universities, and he chooses to matriculate at Yale instead of Harvard for reasons that appear nebulous but soon become entirely obvious, for it is at Yale that James J. Hogan will thrive not just academically, and not just athletically, but also financially.

He plays right tackle on the Yale eleven, and he blossoms into one of the greats of the early-modern era. In 1905, a prominent magazine runs a portrait of Hogan in his team sweater posing up against a fence in a hay pasture, looking like a beefed-up Joaquin Phoenix. Caption: *Yale's football captain, the foremost college athlete of the day.*

Hogan and his quarterback roommate share a suite in Vanderbilt Hall, the most luxurious of the dormitories. He has a one-hundred-dollar scholarship and his tuition is paid in full. He takes his meals at the University Club, an expensive and exclusive outfit that occasionally awards scholarships to worthy undergraduates. Following the 1903 season, he and the team's trainer go on a ten-day trip to Cuba that is paid for entirely by the school's athletic association, which is reportedly backed by a $100,000 slush fund. At a New Haven grill room called Mory's, they sell cigarettes known as Turkish Mogul and Egyptian Deities: These are "Hogan's cigarettes," and he asks Mory's to put them on sale, and he evangelizes about these cigarettes to his friends, and he receives a commission on every sale. His classmates, knowing that James J. Hogan comes from nothing, and furthermore knowing that he is a football star, oblige by purchasing Hogan's smokes. A tobacco executive, speaking with the propriety you'd expect from a tobacco executive, explains that the choice of Hogan as a youthful product endorser will soon be expanded to other campuses, that it has proved a satisfactory transaction for both individual and corporation.

"The 'business arrangement' is important only as showing the growth of commercialism in collegiate sport," writes a muckraking reporter named Henry Beech Needham, in a magazine called *McClure's*. It is the summer of 1905, and soon enough Needham's series of articles about James J. Hogan and others like him, about a game that has become a violent and mercenary enterprise, fall into the hands of Theodore Roosevelt, the president of the United States. And amid this rising tide of violence and corruption, the question arises as to whether the sport of college football has spun hopelessly out of control. Not for the first time, and not for the last time.

II.

It was born into a perpetual state of crisis: A game that was less an organized pastime and more of a primitive hazing ritual, a game so charged with anarchic violence that this appeared to be its sole reason for being. At Harvard, they referred to the yearly freshman-sophomore melee as "Bloody Monday" until it was outlawed altogether by the faculty in 1860; at Yale, they sang couplets about tearing shirts and britches and ripping stitches. The lone objective was to advance an inflated pig's bladder toward a goal, and the rules varied from moment to moment and from field to field. It was a disjointed hybrid of soccer and rugby and *The Hunger Games;* more often than not in those early years, with a nation on the brink of Civil War, it devolved into something unsightly and unruly and occasionally fatal. "The game consisted of kicking, pushing, slugging," wrote author Allison Danzig, "and getting angry."

These are the origins of college football as we know it; it is a sport that had to be actively tamed from the moment of its origin.

Officially, we can trace it back to November 6, 1869, to a cow pasture along College Avenue in New Brunswick, New Jersey: Twenty-five men to a side, the playing field 360 feet long and 225 feet wide. The ball was round, but it kept deflating and the participants took turns blowing it back up again, and so its shape was often ambiguous. Points were scored by booting it between a pair of vertical posts. The rules were aligned most closely with European soccer, and the men stripped off their waistcoats and tied turbans around their heads. Somebody on the Rutgers side, whose shame will forever remain anonymous, accidentally scored on his own goal. A Princeton player called Big Mike was assigned to break up the opposition's ball protectors by burrowing straight through them; at one point, he and a Rutgers opponent wrestled over a loose ball and crashed headlong into a board fence on which several spectators were perched, toppling the fence and everyone on it.

"You men will come to no Christian end!" shouted a Rutgers professor, as he happened past on his bicycle.

Rutgers won 6–4, and then, by at least one (perhaps apocryphal) account, they ran the Princeton players straight out of town, sending them hastening toward their wagons and carriages, hence marking the intercollegiate debut of a sport whose caretakers have spent every year since then attempting to sow order from the seeds of barbarism.

III.

The first person to attempt to impose his will on college football was a Yale man named Walter Camp, a noted scholar, a prolific writer, and a fierce proselytizer for the sport. Camp played his football in New Haven, and then stayed around for decades afterward, working as an executive at the New England Clock Company. He was a bulwark on the early football rules committees and within the fledgling organizations that shaped the sport. It was Walter Camp who first suggested that a team should be composed of eleven men rather than fifteen, thereby shedding at least a measure of the sport's unruliness, and it was Walter Camp who devised the most crucial early change of all: the idea of a "scrimmage" rather than a "scrum," the idea that football should be carefully demarcated into plays, the idea that it should be about the gradual acquisition of territory rather than a chaotic and constant jostling for position. It was Walter Camp who first molded football from a European rugby hybrid into a uniquely American enterprise rooted in manifest destiny; it was Walter Camp who imposed corporate bureaucracy onto the game, demarcating positions and responsibilities; it was Walter Camp who rescued college football, and it was Walter Camp who nearly presided over its demise.

By then, Camp had established Yale as the Ivy League's preeminent college football program, which meant, at the time, that Yale was also the nation's preeminent college football program. The sport didn't technically have coaches yet, and any sort of in-game counsel was considered a shady pursuit, in keeping with the British tradition of letting players act freely during the contests themselves; in fact, sideline coaching was not officially sanctioned until 1967, but I think it is fair to say that Camp was the man who laid down the template for what a football coach could be, at least in terms of bureaucratic micromanagement and metaphors about manhood. He wrote books loaded with language that has now become cliché. (Subject headings in 1896's *Football,* under Chapter VIII: The Moral Factors In An Important Game: *Comparison Between War and Football, Napoleon's "Three to One" Ratio, The Qualifications of Generalship, Force of Strategy in Football, The Elation or Depression of the Soldiers.* Sample quote: "But football games are not won or lost by luck, except in very rare instances. What appears to be luck is inevitably some of the moral qualities here enumerated, which, carefully nurtured by one coach, and perhaps unapprehended or unappreciated by the opponents, proves to be a turning-point in the contest.")

His ideas were sometimes contradictory and occasionally self-interested: At least once, he manipulated data in one of his own texts in order to make football appear less violent than it actually was. His tomes included extensive treatises on play-calling and curfew times and "increasing nitrogenous ratio." He published a detailed chart on the digestion time of certain foods, which discouraged the consumption of fried beef hearts less than four hours before game time. He believed his players should drink beer and not tea, for therapeutic reasons. He believed they should consume a glass of cold water every morning, and that they should smoke only after breakfasting on stale bread.

Camp was raised in an era of renewed emphasis on physical fitness, an era when industrial advances were calling into question the idea of what it meant to be a man.[1] For Camp, football bridged that gap. For Camp, football was a potent link between the college life and corporate life, a training ground for future executives who wished to become cogs in the machinery of society. And so he bent the rules to fit the experiment (and often, the strengths of his own teams). Camp's rules made football less of a spontaneous bloodthirsty orgy and more of a hypercontrolled scientific enterprise. It was now more about work than it was about fun, and this became the ethic of every coach who followed him: *Football would be rewarding precisely because it was so severely proscribed. Football was about manufacturing masculinity.*

Control—of the ball, of the game, of the perception of football among the general public—was everything. Control, in Walter Camp's eyes, was what separated football from savagery. "It is true that the tendency of the game is toward roughness," Camp wrote, "but this tendency may be quickly checked by competent officials."

And so Camp's precepts were widely adopted, and the college game spread throughout the Northeast and into the Midwest, and it was right around this time, just as football pushed its way into the mainstream of American culture, that people began to die.

---

1. In his book *The Big Scrum: How Teddy Roosevelt Saved Football,* John J. Miller refers to the influence of a children's book called *Tom Brown's Schooldays,* which advocated the use of physical violence in passages like this: "From the cradle to the grave, fighting, rightly understood, is the business, the real, high honestest business of every son of man."

IV.

"The game Camp created, his vision of its place in American life,
kept slipping away from him."

—Michael Oriard, *Reading Football*

V.

Charles Eliot was an awkward child, burdened by a birthmark on
his face and a crippling case of nearsightedness. In some ways, he
was the archetypal nerd: He was fifteen when he entered Harvard,
and at thirty-five he became the school's president, a position he
remained in for forty years. He was detached and aloof, and he
believed in the importance of a rigorous physical education but
found the notion of team sports immoral. "A game that needs to
be watched [by umpires and referees] is not fit for genuine sports-
men," he said, and he worried most of all about football, about
the way it caused students to neglect their studies, about its star
system, about the escalation in violence that had come to define
it in the popular press. In 1885, Harvard experimented with ban-
ning football for a year, then quickly rescinded the ban. In 1894,
after an especially savage battle with Yale, Harvard temporarily
suspended the rivalry.

Eliot believed that sports distracted from Harvard's academic
mission; he believed that football produced an "unwholesome
desire for victory," that it would only become increasingly dangerous, that it encouraged men to injure each other for no apparent
reason. The problem for Charles Eliot—and the problem for all

the critics of college football who followed him—was that the sport seemed *designed* to inflict injury, and this became the Rorschach test for college football: Either you believed it could be tamed and utilized for the common good, or you found it barbaric and pointless and inherently evil in the first place. On a college campus, in an institution of higher learning, there would always be an essential divide between men like Charles Eliot and men like Walter Camp. It was proto-nerds versus jocks, *Revenge of the Nerds* in knickers.

Hence the nation's two most prestigious universities stood in opposition: Harvard became the voice of "Puritan intolerance," as embodied by Charles Eliot; Yale became the voice of "pragmatic modernity," as embodied by Walter Camp. And this became the first great college football rivalry, and remains perhaps the most venerated rivalry today, all because it grew up around the question of whether the sport should exist at all.

VI.

But now people were dying. This wasn't exactly a new thing, given how obdurate those who played the game have always been to the idea of restraint. From the earliest days, people had died while playing football—the very idea of padding and helmetry remained a fledgling concept, and shaggy hair was considered the best protection against concussion. But by the late nineteenth century the *perception* of death and football had changed, in part because of the proliferation of mass media reporting on the sport (a newspaper sports section was now a common thing), and in part because of an innovation known as the "flying wedge," a simple and deadly offensive formation that consisted of seven blockers gathering into a solid, V-shaped torpedo of human muscle in order to protect a rusher and inflict maximal damage on defenders who stood in the way.

This, along with Camp's idea of legalizing tackling below the waist, led to the popularity of "momentum mass" plays, linemen launching themselves forward from a spot well behind the line of scrimmage in order to open a hole for the ballcarrier like a formation of angry birds. And this is when organized football sank back to its primacy: Femurs shattered, and skulls were broken, and men bled upon each other, and even after the flying wedge was outlawed, the momentum mass playbook remained. In 1905, a Union College player named Harold Moore died while trying to make a tackle against New York University; that same season, Columbia chose to ban football, and a Harvard player had his nose deliberately broken while fielding a punt against Yale. A total of eighteen people died playing football in 1905, according to official accounts, and while only three of them were actually playing college football when they died, the Ivies were the most visible, especially in the Northeast. Violence begat violence, and the culture soon deteriorated: When a Dartmouth player (who was black) suffered a broken collarbone, someone accused the Princeton player who had inflicted the injury of racism.

"We didn't put him out because he is a black man," the Princeton player replied. "We're coached to pick out the most dangerous man on the opposing side and put him out in the first five minutes of the game."

Offenses had closed up, since this seemed the best way to

advance through territory, and plays ended in mass pileups and near brawls, and this was where Walter Camp, who firmly believed that brains would organically overcome brawn, had gone wrong: The game required intellectual control to be imposed on it, but the point of controlling it was to suppress its primal nature. Suddenly, the game had been legislated to the point where it was deadly *and* boring.

And at the same time, it was also becoming inherently corrupt.

VII.

"It is obvious that no student should be paid for his athletics. The practice of assisting young men through college in order that they may strengthen the athletic teams is degrading to amateur sport."

—conclusion of the Conference of Intercollegiate Athletics, Brown University, February 18, 1898

VIII.

College football had been fully institutionalized by 1905, but it still adhered to the same standards: Because it had grown out of the Ivy League, and because it could still be traced back to those spontaneous expositions of youthful enthusiasm on the campus green, nobody really imagined why it should be anything *but* an amateur pursuit. By the time of Henry Beech Needham's *McClure's* exposé, crowds often swelled into the tens of thousands, and football had become intertwined with the identity of the university itself.

Already, the game seemed almost indispensable, and colleges were making too much money to loosen the control they'd exacted over it. "Once they took over the previously renegade sports programs, university officials went heavy on the Olympic Ideal business as handed over from England because they could see that big-time, revenue-producing sport had no place in the collegiate world and therefore needed very careful justification to exist on campus," wrote author Rick Telander in his 1989 book, *The Hundred-Yard Lie.* "The concept of amateurism gave the university brass this justification, as it still does today."

Telander advocated for an upheaval of the entire system, but in 1905, Needham argued only that the amateur ideal should be upheld, and that the adults should further seize hold of the situation before college football became something incompatible with the Campian ideal. He noted the plague of "proselytizing, or the recruiting to which public school subjects are currently subjected," and the growth of "a class of students tainted with commercialism"; he told the story of James J. Hogan at Yale, and of Andrew L. Smith, who played for Pennsylvania State College one week and the University of Pennsylvania the next, then, after enrolling in classes at Penn, played three more games for Penn State. Needham lamented that the growth of all these elements would inevitably signal the end of amateurism. "Who can blame the college man for harboring the desire to win? No one," he wrote. "But it is more than that: to win at any cost—that is the source of the present deplorable condition of intercollegiate athletics."

This notion of fair play appealed to Teddy Roosevelt's sense of morality; if football was designed to mold boys into men, how could it be also tainted by violent excess and commercialism?

Soon after Needham's articles ran, Roosevelt gave a commencement speech at Harvard, intertwining bad business behavior with the excesses of college football.

It's not really clear whether college football was truly on the verge of being outlawed at that moment, or if the media merely forced a reexamination of the sport by counting the number of deaths. If so, it wasn't Roosevelt who would have outlawed it, in part because he didn't have the power to do it, and in part because he didn't want to do it. He possessed a hearty contempt for those who considered a misshapen forearm or a shattered collarbone "as of serious consequence, when balanced against the chance of showing that he possesses hardihood, physical address, and courage." He still believed in football, even as the critics lined up against it, even as Charles Eliot published a report titled "THE EVILS OF FOOTBALL." The game's rules, Eliot wrote, were entirely unenforceable precisely because the game itself was designed to seize on the worst of human nature; it was based in deceit and its anarchistic spirit was precisely akin to war, and it should be euthanized before it could prosper any further.

"I think Harvard will be doing the baby act if she takes any such foolish course as President Eliot advises!" Roosevelt wrote in a letter. He summoned Camp, along with representatives from Harvard and Princeton, to the White House; months later, after the death of Union's Harold Moore during that game against NYU, a conference of top schools was held in New York. None of the three major Ivy League programs showed up. Systemically, Camp's power was usurped, and the Intercollegiate Athletic Association was formed to govern the game. Five years later, this governing body's name was changed to the National Collegiate

Athletic Association. This NCAA was charged with restoring order to a sport that, as if driven by genetic imperative, seems to reflexively rebel against it.

IX.

And so a growing number of reformers came to understand that the game needed to edge toward freedom and open space without degrading back into chaos. Amid the byzantine and frequent football politicking of the mid-aughts, under the loose supervision of Roosevelt himself, Camp suggested extending a first down from five yards to ten. A neutral zone between offense and defense was established, and then a rules change was adopted that Camp did not approve of at all: the legalization of the forward pass.

As with much of football's early history, the question of who threw the first forward pass is mired in a series of dubious historical accounts, but for all we know, it may have actually been Walter Camp himself: During an 1876 game between Princeton and Yale, Camp hurled the bladder forward to a teammate named Oliver Thompson, who scrambled downfield for a touchdown. Princeton protested; a flummoxed referee tossed a coin to decide, and he ruled in favor of Yale. Then in 1895, John Heisman, coaching at Auburn, saw a punter for North Carolina take a snap, step to his right, and throw a seventy-yard touchdown, after which Georgia coach Glenn Warner protested and the referee declared that since he had somehow failed to see it at all, the play would stand. Heisman found it a fascinating development; he became one of the chief evangelists of the forward pass. For nearly another decade after its adoption, no one could quite figure out the best way to utilize it, at least until an insignificant little Catholic college called Notre Dame used it to defeat Army in 1913. But it succeeded immediately in altering the perception of football.

It's impossible, I think, to overstate the impact of the forward pass: I might argue that, other than the automobile, it was the single most important American invention of the early twentieth century. It permitted the American game a tool to continue evolving, and to offset its animalistic roots (at least in a visual sense). That it took decades before the forward pass was regarded as a "manly pursuit"—that this line of thinking is still advanced in disputes among intoxicated male sports-bar patrons—is proof of its progressiveness. Even Charles Eliot at Harvard admitted that football was "somewhat improved" after 1905.

I'm not entirely sure why Camp disdained the pass so much, but it seems at least partly based on the reasons that conservative coaches disdained the forward pass for decades afterward: It felt risky and hypermodern. It was dangerous in the way that football wasn't *supposed* to be dangerous; when it was first legalized, I'm sure it felt like a way of (both literally and figuratively) cheating death. I imagine Walter Camp must have felt that tossing the ball skyward rather than crashing headlong through a wall of defenders was a cheap shortcut around the barricades that football erected, that it glorified the individual over the team, and that it was yet another example of the corrosion of the American work ethic. I imagine the pass broke down the metaphor of football in Camp's mind, and I imagine that thinkers like Walter Camp begat generations of scrupulous coaches who declared that only three things could happen when you threw the ball, and two of them were bad. I imagine that the conceptions Camp set down for football explain why in 2012, more than a hundred years after the adoption of the forward pass, Alabama coach Nick Saban— the modern incarnation of the Campian control-freak micro-manager—lodged an extended complaint about how pass-heavy hurry-up offenses might alter the game in ways that defied its basic spirit. ("I just think there's got to be some sense of fairness in terms of asking, Is this what we want football to be?" Saban said.)

Whatever it was, Walter Camp would not change his mind about it until it was abundantly clear that the forward pass had become the best thing that had ever happened to the sport. And by then, what Camp thought no longer mattered. As the twenti-eth century progressed, he felt himself losing control: The game, now spreading west, was no longer in the hands of the northeast-ern elite; the tenor of it was now dictated by the mass media and by the spectators, many of whom never quite got it before the forward pass opened it up to them. "With the wave of popularity that has seized upon all forms of athletic sport," Camp wrote, "the spectator has become a great problem."

Camp died in 1925, in New York City, while attending a meeting of football's rules committee. The forward pass endured.

X.

Of course, the raging commercialism that struck such fear into Henry Beech Needham and Theodore Roosevelt did not actu-ally prefigure the death of anything. College football is still here, and amateurism is still here, and they have clung to an uneasy coexistence through decades of social and technological evolution that have engendered spectacularly creative methods of corruption. (By now, corruption is an integral part of college football; I might argue that the colorful nature of it all lends the sport almost as much character as, say, the marching band does.) Amateurism endures because it is what Walter Camp envisioned, in all his paternalistic glory, and it endures because it serves as a thinly veiled defense mechanism against critics like Charles Eliot. It is a method of controlling perception: Once college football becomes an unapologetic business enterprise, what possible case can be made that it should be lashed to a college in the first place?

Certain things have changed since 1905. Geography, for instance: The game does not belong to the place of its roots anymore. Harvard and Yale play football mostly so they can maintain traditions and perpetrate elaborate pranks on each other's student bodies. Still, college football remains a perpetual dilemma, and the dilemma remains fundamentally the same: There are those who seek new ways to maintain control over the beast, and there are those who wish to set it free. There are the liberals, and there are the conservatives, and the only way college football can possibly survive is if these elements remain in constant opposition.

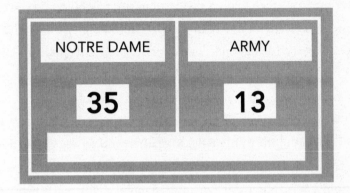

NOTRE DAME	ARMY
35	13

November 1, 1913

Like a Prayer

Discussion Topics: Catholicism • Hebrew School • Shitting on Pitt •
Imaginary Girlfriends • Brigham Young University • The Gipper •
Faith • Superstition

I.

I learned to hate Notre Dame in the early 1980s, and I can assure you it had nothing to do with Catholicism, because at that point in my life, I didn't have any idea what Catholicism was, or what it might possibly have to do with something as spectacularly awesome as college football. All I knew was that there were two monolithic American faiths, and the children of the predominant faith were required to attend something called "church" on sporadic Sundays

in exchange for receiving the whole of the Sears catalog on Christ-
mas Eve; and the children of the minority faith (my own) were
sentenced to attend ninety minutes of stultifying Hebrew School
lectures every Tuesday and Thursday afternoon at the Jewish Community Center on Hamilton Avenue in exchange for receiving a
six-pack of tube socks on the first night of Chanukah.

When Penn State began a yearly series with Notre Dame in
1981, I was in the third grade. My father worked at a public university, and my life was pretty much centered around that public university, but I did not understand the difference between
public colleges and private colleges any better than I did the difference between Protestants and Catholics.[1] I didn't know that
Notre Dame was a private Catholic school steeped in religious
symbolism; I didn't know that they fielded the most polarizing
team in college football, and I didn't know that they trafficked on
a curious amalgam of nostalgia and mysticism that dated back to
the early twentieth century. To me, Notre Dame was just another
rival, the kind of rival you learned to dislike instinctively, because
they were at the tail end of the schedule every year, dovetailed
with longtime foil Pittsburgh,[2] and because they fielded reason-
ably competitive teams even when it seemed like they shouldn't.

For most of my childhood, my parents had season tickets in
the fifth row at Penn State games, directly behind the visitors'
bench. You could glean certain things about the opponent merely
by noting the makeup of that sideline—Temple and Rutgers,

---

1. Actually, I still don't know the difference between Protestants and Catholics.

2. My first exposure to the power of the profane insult in college football: the
mustard-yellow "Shitt on Pitt" buttons Penn State fans used to affix to their lapels
like protest slogans.

sparse and scrawny; Nebraska and Iowa, midsections bulging with excess corn-weight—but it was the secondary adornments that set Notre Dame apart: The gilded helmets, the mascot who appeared to have sprung full-form out of a box of Lucky Charms, the nickname appropriated from an ethnic slur, and the fan base, which seemed nebulous and omnipresent and only loosely connected to the university itself. I'd see the ND flags draped over the wraparound porches on houses when driving through the industrial towns in my home state, in places like Scranton and Berwick and Reading, and I'd have trouble grasping why Notre Dame seemed to accumulate support in places like this when the local state university *was right here.*

So, yes, I admit I did not like Notre Dame because they were an "other." This tendency to tribalize without thought, I suppose, is both the pleasure and the danger of growing up in a sports-addled college community like mine. But I had no idea what Notre Dame's "otherness" signified; I had no idea that this "otherness" was the very thing that had elevated Notre Dame into a national symbol in the first place.

II.

"A large part of Notre Dame's subsequent football fame, and the fervent support of huge numbers of middle-class and poor Catholics for the Fighting Irish, resulted from these clashes with—and triumphs over—opponents claiming superiority in class and wealth."

—Murray Sperber, *Shake Down the Thunder*

III.

In November 1842, the representatives of a French religious order called the Congregation of the Holy Cross stumbled upon a tract of land at the south bend of the St. Joseph's River in Indiana. Here, in the middle of nowhere, they founded a college, and they called it Notre Dame, and they attracted the sons of working-class Catholics and of Irish immigrants who made their way to the fertile plains of the Midwest in the wake of the potato famine. It would take nearly fifty years for the school to get serious about football; in 1896, when Michigan joined up with a sporting collective known as the Western Conference (the godmother of the Big Ten), Notre Dame lobbied for admission. They were rejected. They were told their enrollment was too small, but they understood the real reason: They were seen, according to author Ray Robinson, as a " 'slum college,' with loose eligibility rules—just a bunch of low-life Catholics trying to get ahead in the world."

And then in 1910, the most impactful recruit in Notre Dame history, a prematurely balding twenty-two-year-old Protestant of Norwegian descent (by way of Chicago) enrolled as a freshman. It is difficult to glean the straight story on Knute Rockne's undergraduate career at Notre Dame, but here are a few facts:

- Rockne's first roommate at Sorin Hall, quarterback Gus Dorais, would later become the other half of a tandem that would come to invent the forward pass;
- The first time Rockne went out for football as a freshman end, he froze while trying to punt, so he was yanked out of

the game and sent home. He was, he later said, a washout, "not even good enough for the scrubs";

- Rockne persevered, and after Notre Dame's unprecedented aerial display in an upset of Army in 1913, he became a local hero. "Everybody in the school, save the older professors, wanted to be a football player," he said. "I recall even Cy Williams, the home-run slugger with the Philadelphia Nationals, clamoring for football togs. But the baseball coach barred Cy from football, afraid that Cy might get hurt."

IV.

I should pause here for a correction: None of what I've written above is entirely true.

This happens quite often when exploring the Rockne legend: Fact and fantasy get so twisted that it becomes almost impossible to extricate one from the other. According to Ray Robinson's 1999 book, *Rockne of Notre Dame,* Cy Williams, the baseball slugger Rockne mentions, had already graduated, and had already played for the Chicago Cubs; he was also serving as the school's baseball coach in 1913, which meant he would have somehow banned himself from something he was no longer eligible to do. Rockne did not live in Sorin Hall as a freshman, and Gus Dorais did not become his roommate until much later in their Notre Dame careers, although the introduction to Rockne's own autobiography—as well as a scene in the hagiographic film *Knute Rockne: All-American,* in which puggish actor Pat O'Brien, as Rockne, tries to convince us he is not actually forty years old—

presents the details of this more convenient narrative as fact. And Rockne did not struggle as a freshman, even if he liked to spread self-deprecating tales about himself: In his first game, he was a starter, and he hit the opposing line so hard that the local newspaper wrote he "would make a billy goat blush with envy."

It *is* true that Notre Dame's win over Army—highlighted by several throws from Dorais to Rockne, a skill they practiced while working at an Ohio amusement park called Cedar Point that summer[3]—was a turning point for the forward pass in football. But it is entirely untrue, as many seem to think, that Knute Rockne was somehow responsible for the invention of the forward pass.[4] The forward pass existed years before Rockne popularized it among the Northeast media during that game at West Point; he just turned it into an aspirational equalizer for football programs from coast to coast. By the time Rockne showed up on campus, the Fighting Irish already had adopted their ubiquitous Victory March, and they had already defeated Michigan in 1909, and they had already recruited athletes from at least twelve states, raising questions about whether this "slum college" might also be bending the rules.

So it's very possible that Notre Dame would have become "Notre Dame" in some altered form without Rockne—that the Fighting Irish were already on an inextricable path toward

---

3. On one memorable play, Rockne faked a limp, convincing the opposing halfback that he wasn't even worth watching as a decoy, and then sprinted downfield and caught a forty-yard touchdown pass. Was this deceptive? Yes. Was it effective? Absolutely.

4. In fact, as I write this, the lead customer review on Amazon.com for *Knute Rockne: All-American* declares "there is little doubt that Rockne invented the forward pass." This, despite the fact that the film—which stretches the truth to its breaking point in nearly every scene—is careful never to actually make this claim.

national prominence through football by the time he came along. But Knute Rockne is still the most important figure in school history (if not the entire history of the sport), because he elevated college football into a choreographed theatrical experience.

"Rockne regarded football as drama and the squad as a cast," wrote journalist Edwin Pope, "and, in essence, he tried to make a practice field out of both the practice field and the stadium, to keep both spectators and participants entertained at all times."

And he was so skillful at perpetuating these things—at engendering faith in a manufactured inspirational tale—that it's pretty much impossible, a hundred years on, to imagine what college football would look like without him.

V.

"So what is so fantastic about the Manti Te'o story? . . . It's *Love Story* meets Icarus meets inspirational outsider. It wasn't enough that Manti's love affair be doomed, that his girlfriend had leukemia, and that he drew from her death the inspiration to go out and get 12 tackles in the crucial defeat of Michigan State. *She also had to be severely injured in a car accident.*"

—Malcolm Gladwell, on Grantland.com

VI.

In October 2012, a few months before the muckraking sports website Deadspin published a story headlined "Manti Te'o's Dead

Girlfriend, The Most Heartbreaking And Inspirational Story Of
The College Football Season, Is A Hoax," I stood on a promenade
near the Notre Dame campus library and gazed up at a mural of a
haloed Jesus, arms outstretched above a gaudy no-huddle formation of saints. The mural's official designation is *The Word of Life,*
but I had no idea what its official designation was until I looked
it up, because I'd only known it from afar, for all these years, as
Touchdown Jesus. You can bear witness to *Touchdown Jesus* from
the press box, and from most of the seats in the low-slung bowl
of Notre Dame Stadium; it is perhaps the most overt marriage of
football and faith in America outside of Tim Tebow's cerebellum.
I was there for a game between Brigham Young University and
undefeated Notre Dame, and the plaza in front of the library was
crowded with true believers, Christians and Mormons intermingling with at least one lonely secular Jew. People took photos with
their arms raised in bemused supplication, and a gang of well-
lubricated Notre Dame students charged through the mud and
grass and packs of gridiron tourists toward a stadium gate adorned
with a statue of Knute Rockne himself.

That same day, the local newspaper, the *South Bend Tribune,*
published a story about BYU fans who had journeyed to Notre
Dame especially for this football game. This happens every home
weekend in South Bend—one of the reasons Notre Dame football
crowds are not particularly loud is that many in attendance are
first-time visitors who are gawking at their surroundings—but I
suppose the religious undertones, and the peaceable intermingling
of two of America's most prominent faiths, elevated this story to
front-page news. The whole thing played out like a revival, like
you couldn't possibly leave here without rediscovering faith in

something, even if it was only in Mitt Romney's floundering presidential campaign.

The *Sports Illustrated* writer Dan Jenkins once referred to the Notre Dame campus as "self-haunting," and everywhere, in case you'd left your sepia-filter glasses at home, there were blatant and over-the-top reminders that this is a place like no other: My press pass was adorned with silhouettes of the Four Horsemen, and on my way back from *Touchdown Jesus,* I passed statues of both Rockne and Lou Holtz. For a long time, dating back to the Holtz squads of the late 1980s and early 1990s (the last Notre Dame teams to contend for a national championship before the 2012 season, the teams I hated so fiercely as a teenager), all that history had become more of a sinkweight than a cudgel.

But it appeared to me, in the fall of 2012, like something both mystical and mythological was taking place, amid Notre Dame's 125th season of football. At that point, the Irish were undefeated, and their defense hadn't given up a touchdown in more than a month; they would wind up beating several good teams, and outlasting Stanford in overtime on at least two controversial calls, reinforcing the notion that this Irish team was a throwback to the days when all that history actually counted for something. They would finish their regular season 12-0, and they would play Alabama for a national championship, which, given where the program had been—given that Notre Dame had suffered a two-decades series of humiliations related to both its coaches[5] and players—felt like something of a miracle in itself.

---

5. One of them, George O'Leary, was fired five days after being hired, for falsifying his resume. Another, Charlie Weis, the former offensive coordinator of the New England Patriots, alienated virtually the entire fan base with his cartoonish egotism.

And at the heart of that miracle: Manti Te'o, the Mormon Hawaiian linebacker who was dating a beautiful Stanford coed, though said coed had been injured in a car crash, and then had contracted leukemia, and then died within forty-eight hours of Te'o's grandmother.[6] Manti Te'o, who had persevered through all of that to become the quiet embodiment of this Notre Dame revival, telling a national television reporter after the win over Michigan State that his girlfriend and his grandmother were with him the whole time. Manti Te'o, who had ten tackles and an interception as Notre Dame eked past BYU 17–14 that afternoon.

"We're no longer crossing our fingers," Te'o told me afterward, when I asked him about Notre Dame's tendency to succumb to collapse and/or catastrophe in recent years. "We're no longer waiting for the other shoe to drop."

VII.

The real George Gipp was not a paragon of American virtue. The real George Gipp was not a gentle young soul who hid out from the media at coach Rockne's house after games and palled around with his children (as does a young Ronald Reagan, playing Gipp, in *Knute Rockne: All-American*—a role that he trafficked on through five decades of public life). The real George Gipp was not referred to, except on rare occasions, as the Gipper.

The real George Gipp was a gambler and a carouser, a loose cannon who hung out at pool halls and with men Ray Robinson

---

6. In retrospect, it *does* seem kind of stupid that we ever took his word on this.

refers to as "downtown cronies." When Rockne laid into him during practice, Gipp would refuse to suit up and meander off to
a convenient poker game. He was a tremendous halfback who
didn't much seem to care about the true purpose of higher education: He was named team captain at the end of 1919, and was
expelled from school in 1920. When he was recruited by Michigan and Pittsburgh and the University of Detroit, Rockne lobbied
local leaders, who in turn lobbied Notre Dame president James
Burns, ensuring him that a first-rate football team was a necessity
for maintaining the local economy. And a month after he'd been
expelled, George Gipp was reinstated.[7]

Gipp continued to carouse, and to gamble, and to drink heavily; there is a story about a halftime pep talk Rockne gave during
the 1920 Army game, which Gipp listened to while sitting in a
corner of the locker room, smoking a cigarette. And when Rockne
said, "You, Mr. Gipp, I guess you don't care if we win or lose,"
Gipp stared down his coach and insisted that yes, he *did* care,
because he had five hundred dollars wagered on this game.

This story may be untrue, but one of Gipp's teammates told
Ray Robinson that there was little doubt his teammate wagered
on games, because they all wagered on games (which contrasts
with the image of Rockne shooing a loudly dressed gambler who
shows up in his locker room in *Knute Rockne: All-American,*
bragging about point spreads). Notre Dame did beat Army on
the day that Rockne supposedly challenged Gipp, and then
they beat Purdue, and then they beat Indiana, extending their

---

7. The rumor was that Gipp had taken some sort of rigorous exam for readmission
and had passed with flying colors. This rumor does not appear to be based in fact.

unbeaten streak to seventeen games, Gipp reportedly playing through a dislocated shoulder and a broken collarbone that may or may not have been contracted in the midst of a late-night fit of carousing. Notre Dame won, 13–10, and Gipp got off the train in Chicago and "went on a drinking binge for several days," according to Robinson; by the time he got back to South Bend, he had a sore throat and a fever (and apparently a streptococcus infection).

This is where *Knute Rockne: All-American* picks things up— with Rockne examining Gipp's throat himself in front of a roaring fire, declaring him severely ill, and sending him straight to the ER. And then, suddenly, the Gipper is dying young amid the bleary white light of a hospital room set, and Ronald Reagan is delivering the most famous valedictory in college football history:

> What's so tough about it? I've got to go, Rock. It's all right. I'm not afraid. Sometimes when things are going wrong, when the breaks are beating the boys, tell them to go out and win one for the Gipper. I don't know where I'll be then, Rock, but I'll know about it and I'll be happy.

Did George Gipp actually utter these words? Unknown. There are believers, and there are nonbelievers, but there's enough prefabricated hokum in Rockne's oeuvre that it's kind of hard to believe he would wait *eight years* to share these words with anyone around him, and would choose to do so during halftime of a particularly dramatic Army game at Yankee Stadium in 1928. And yet *Knute Rockne: All-American* made it part of the canon. And *Knute Rockne: All-American,* with its rousing portrayals of campus life and sports and of the high-minded college coach, became the Platonic ideal of intercollegiate football.

It was shrewd, what Rockne did, and for a long time it worked in Notre Dame's favor: College football is a sport whose champion is chosen by opinion polls, and from the mid-1930s until the late 1960s, the only relevant poll was the Associated Press poll, which happened to be dominated by the same New York sportswriters who had grown up as Rockne admirers and as Subway Alumni[8] in the mid-1920s and beyond. Most claims of bias in sports are empty and partisan whines, but for a long time—up through at least the early 1990s—there really *was* a pro–Notre Dame bias, because of the foundation Rockne had laid with big-city columnists like Grantland Rice, whose overwrought account of Rockne's "Four Horsemen" backfield in 1924 is still the most famous sports article of the twentieth century.

"*Knute Rockne: All-American* is the cinematic equivalent of Grantland Rice's prose," wrote author Murray Sperber, "and even its depiction of the 1920s' press attention to Notre Dame football—a sudden whirring of newspaper printing machines and spewing of front-page headlines—is characteristically mystified."

So what did it matter, then, if the fabrications served a higher purpose?

In 1922, Notre Dame played at Georgia Tech, and Rockne, in the midst of a rousing pregame speech, extracted a crumpled telegram from his pocket, and read aloud: "PLEASE WIN THIS GAME FOR MY DADDY. IT'S VERY IMPORTANT TO HIM."

---

8. This is the term used to describe the considerable percentage of Notre Dame fans who never attended Notre Dame.

It was, Rockne said, from his six-year-old son Billy, who was ill in the hospital. Some of Rockne's players began to cry; others leapt up and swore they would win that game for the kid if it was the last thing they did. And they did win, 13–3, and when they arrived back at the railroad station, there was Billy Rockne, healthy as a six-year-old kid could possibly be. It was manipulative, and it was deceptive, and it was a blatant exploitation of a young man's faith in his coach. None of them seemed to mind.

VIII.

When the other shoe dropped on Manti Te'o, it fell pretty damned hard. And I'm inclined to believe that his story is exactly what he claimed, once the tabloid fairy dust had cleared; I'm inclined to believe that he did not conspire to create and then murder a woman who never existed, just to enhance his chances of winning the Heisman Trophy, for which he was never more than a long-shot candidate; I'm inclined to believe that he really did have no idea sometime in December 2012, a few weeks before the Deadspin story was published, that his dead girlfriend was a pixelated lie. I'm inclined to believe that he did not know she had apparently been dreamed up by a troubled twenty-two-year-old casual acquaintance named Ronaiah Tuiasosopo, who apparently had fallen in love with Te'o.

I'm going to assume Manti Te'o was a gullible dupe. I'm going to assume this was nothing more than a fascinating (if ultimately harmless) public embarrassment (as much for the media who swallowed it as for Te'o himself), but it was easy to see where the outrage stemmed from: In a matter of hours after Deadspin posted its story, Te'o became the proxy for everything that people have *always* hated about Notre Dame, about the sense of entitlement and self-promotion and self-generated mystique that Knute Rockne once utilized to combat the very real anti-Catholic prejudice of the early twentieth century. But now that this prejudice had been marginalized, and now that Notre Dame hadn't contended for a national championship in twenty years, and now that the hero-worshipping media posture that Walter Camp once called "the broad folk highway of the nation" had long since passed, it just struck people as annoying, and kind of stupid—the way it did to me as a kid, when I had all of the exposure to Notre Dame and none of the context.

A week before the Deadspin exposé on Te'o, Notre Dame played Alabama for the national championship in Miami. I was there that night, and I remember thinking the Irish had a real chance. I remember thinking, *Maybe the mythology still means something in this day and age.* And then the game started. And this contest was straight-up over 177 seconds after it started, when Alabama scored a touchdown on the first of several furious topspin corner-pocket bursts by a Crimson Tide tailback. It turned out that I'd been deluding myself about Notre Dame's defense, about their potential to win a game like this with an inexperienced quarterback and no real dynamic on offense; it turned out that Manti Te'o, his mind no doubt occupied by the fact that he'd spent his summer dating a spectre, was hardly present at all that night.

Alabama won 42–14. It was nowhere near that close.

One hundred years after Dorais hurled that touchdown pass to an injury-feinting Rockne at West Point, it felt like Notre Dame's cultural hegemony was in decline, their nationwide fan base slowly peeling off. They were still the only program with an entire television network (NBC) at their disposal, but they no longer had unfettered access to the Catholic recruiting litter; a series of coaches had arrived in South Bend with high hopes and left humiliated, and now, despite a near-perfect season, the Alabama thrashing had negated it all, and the Te'o story had compounded their embarrassment.

Oddly, I found myself pulling hard for Notre Dame in 2012, if only because I wanted them to belong again—if only because I realized, for the first time, that college football was *better* with Notre Dame in it. And when they lost, and when the Te'o story broke, I felt kind of guilty for buying in to any of it in the first place. But I guess we all did.

IX.

So I don't really despise Notre Dame the way I did in the 1980s, largely because it's much easier to stop hating when neither your school nor your rivals are as formidable as they used to be. But I also no longer hate Notre Dame because I think they represent the fundamental contradiction of what it means to be a college football fan: You're placing your faith in something that is rationally unsound. We know that the Rockne myth was largely based on canards and half-truths; we know that he played professional football on the sly to make extra money while he was still enrolled at Notre Dame, and that he endorsed Studebaker automobiles (among other things), and that his recruiting tactics were so underhanded, according to assistant (and future Irish head coach) Frank Leahy, that they would have "appall[ed] a modern coach." We know that the *Knute Rockne: All-American* archetype was not the truth, but this was what we came to believe college football *could* be. This was the pipe dream; this is still the pipe dream. And so, as one of Rockne's equally fanciful contemporaries wrote, we beat on, boats against the current.

When I think back to those Penn State–Notre Dame games in the 1980s, I recall one moment in particular. I can't remember what year it was, or what the score was; all I know is that Penn State was playing at Notre Dame Stadium, and the Nittany Lions were ahead in the fourth quarter, and I was watching, as I often did, by myself, in the finished basement of my parents' house on Devonshire Drive, a small room with wood walls and pea soup carpet and a thirteen-inch black-and-white television. I prefer to watch Penn State games alone; Hebrew School never stuck for me, and so those three hours are the closest thing I have to a religious experience in adulthood.

I was standing next to a chair that day, in an awkward position, when Penn State scored a touchdown. And for at least an hour, I did not move my body at all. My feet fell asleep, and my arms began to ache, and my nose itched, and my bladder swelled, and I wanted nothing more than to *move*, but I did not. I held completely still. Even at age ten or eleven or whatever I was, I knew this was patently ridiculous—I had a fleeting moment where I wondered if I might somehow paralyze myself—but it felt important to me, to suspend my disbelief, to buy completely in to the irrational faith that college football engenders. To cling to a position, even if that position made no rational sense. To hold on to my faith until it started to hurt.

I wasn't old enough to understand it then. I'm not sure I'm old enough to understand it now. All I know is that my team won the game, and it was totally worth it.

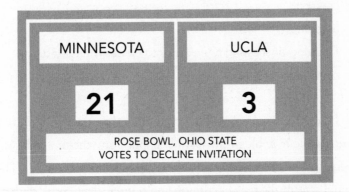

MINNESOTA	UCLA
21	3
ROSE BOWL, OHIO STATE VOTES TO DECLINE INVITATION	

January 1, 1962

An Irascible Man

Discussion Topics: Woody Hayes • Projectiles • Vietnam • Michigan • Sputnik • Cold War Angst • *Slap Shot* • Indoctrination • Rage • Hippies

I.

My father started calling me irascible before I understood what the hell he was talking about. I was eleven, maybe twelve, combative and confused and facing up the ravages of puberty, old enough to sense the pejorative nature of this word he used but not yet immersed in the sufficient level of SAT prep to know the definition. So I went to the dictionary and looked it up:

i·ras·ci·ble

iˈrasəbəl/

adjective

1. having or showing a tendency to be easily angered. "an
   irascible man"

I didn't know many irascible men, other than the father who had
deemed me irascible in the first place, but I saw them on television
every week, and they, as much as my dad, were my role models. They
would scream themselves crimson and mutter silent curses to themselves and throw up their hands in exasperation; they would berate
sideline reporters and shout down officials and drown any sense of
satisfaction in a fury that never seemed to subside. They were football
coaches, and they were the Platonic ideal of irascibility; their irascibility was seen as an essential element of their jobs. And as a kid fighting
the beast inside me, I envied their ability to get away with it.

II.

There are stories of Woody Hayes throwing film projectors and
pitchers of water[1] and first-down markers and cups of coffee and
his own wallet and any other sort of vaguely aerodynamic object he

---

1. His equipment manager used to keep half-a-dozen water pitchers in stock.

could get his hands on, other than an actual football.[2] There are stories of him punching through a blackboard and punching his own players and, during at least one late-night film session that wasn't developing to his liking, punching himself in the face with both fists so hard that he showed up the next day with a pair of black eyes. There are stories of Woody Hayes nearly losing his job as the football coach at New Philadelphia High School in Ohio because he couldn't control his temper. There are stories of a fullback at Denison University, challenging Hayes, his own coach, to a fight right there on the practice field. There are stories of Woody Hayes raging against inefficiency and raging against society and raging against his own inability to stem the tide of generational change.

This is not the complete picture of Woody Hayes, but this is the Woody we remember, the Woody who survives for posterity: He was an irascible man who viewed football as a real live war against the encroaching forces of modernity. It was a war he could not win, but that was never the point. The point was to keep up the goddamned fight, even if it killed you.

III.

In the fall of 1961, in the prime of his career, Woody Hayes's Ohio State Buckeyes opened the season with a 7–7 tie against Texas

---

2. Of all the early- to mid-century coaches who expressed a deep mistrust of the forward pass, Woody may have been the most belligerent; his was the offense that originated the phrase "three yards and a cloud of dust." He did not enjoy the risks that the pass presented. He saw no great need for it. When he got together for an eight-hour session with former coaching rival Sid Gillman, an early progenitor of the passing game, Woody came away saying, "I still don't know what the hell he was talking about."

Christian, and then crushed all their remaining opponents. By that point, Woody had been the coach at Ohio State for a decade, overcoming a rocky early period when, as a relative unknown, he was hired for the job over NFL coaching legend (and Ohio native) Paul Brown. Hayes had won two national championships in the 1950s, and he had established his reputation in Columbus as a pathologically driven conservative ideologue with a furious (and often irrational) temper: Up 48–20 late in the game against a Michigan program he hated so much that he refused to stop in the state to get gas on recruiting trips, Woody rubbed it in by attempting a successful two-point conversion. With that late November victory, the Buckeyes were bound for the Rose Bowl in 1961. And then they weren't.

Late in '61 on the Ohio State campus (and other campuses like it), a dispute broke out over whether, as Woody (and other political conservatives) believed, discipline-driven institutions like college football were exactly what we needed to compete against a country that had launched a canine into space on a Sputnik satellite a few years earlier; or whether, as academicians (and other political liberals) believed, college football had so altered the popular perception of American universities that it had actually become a symbolic threat to our way of life. It was the same essential dilemma that had divided Walter Camp at Yale and Charles Eliot at Harvard in the nineteenth century; it is the same essential dilemma that drives the cable television debate machine of the twenty-first century. *Does college football have a place on a college campus?*

At Ohio State, the debate had been building throughout the 1950s, after the Buckeyes were placed on probation when Hayes admitted he loaned small amounts of money to his own players (who were also being paid through a phony jobs program funded by the local Chamber of Commerce). It was a conflict that reached a fever pitch in the latter half of the decade, after the launch of Sputnik led to a thorough reexamination of American higher education, and after the head of the school's alumni association, Jack Fullen, decided to challenge Hayes's authority. Sputnik elevated the stakes of the Cold War; Sputnik led men like Jack Fullen, once a football booster, to question whether the United States had fallen behind in educating its youth, and to question where major college football fit into that system, at a time when money was tight and faculty salaries were falling. And so in 1961, Ohio State's faculty council voted 28–25 to decline the Rose Bowl invitation.

"It is a way of affirming to the entire world," declared one professor, that his university was "first and last, an institution of higher education, and that athletics are restricted to their properly subordinate place within the structure of the university."

The reaction among the populace was immediate and physical: Thousands of students marched on the president's house, broke windows at the Faculty Club, and burned effigies of Jack Fullen. Woody Hayes, preparing to speak at an alumni function in Cleveland, reportedly "turned gray," and then took an hour-long walk to clear his head. I imagine he spent those sixty minutes waging an intellectual battle against the urge to lash out at something or someone. I imagine those sixty minutes were indicative of the raging war between physical instinct and intellectual restraint that Woody Hayes would wage inside his head for his entire adult life.

IV.

I wasn't big enough or bold enough to play organized football. I played soccer, and I played baseball, and I played neither one particularly well, and when I did play my father was always goading me to be more aggressive but I didn't know how to do it in a real-life context, when faced up against real people. My courage manifested itself when I was alone, in a basement that technically belonged to my parents but essentially belonged to me. I made up names and made up stories and ran through imaginary tackles and shouted and screamed and worked out my anger at my own timidity by crashing against walls and running into chairs and picking fights with opponents who didn't exist. I fell in love with the *idea* of football, with how it looked, with the notion that a sport, especially at the college level, could require both intellect and rigor; I fell in love with the idea of football, even as I understood it was not something that I would ever be able to play.

Most of the time, in my imaginary world, I was a college running back or a quarterback or a linebacker, but on occasion I turned myself into a coach, drawing up plays on the yellow legal pads my father brought home from his office, working my imaginary charges through drills, and screaming them into shape from a sideline only I could see. I was almost a teenager, and I could feel my world changing, and it felt good to lose control and still feel in control of something, even if that something didn't really exist.

V.

Nobody, other than perhaps his friend Richard Nixon, fought imaginary battles with the fervor of Woody Hayes. In the early 1970s, when the Buckeyes went to Berkeley to play Cal, Woody actually whispered his pregame speech in the locker room, fearing that the place had been bugged by hippies. When one of his assistants took his players to see *Easy Rider* the night before a game, Woody grabbed the assistant—who reportedly thought the film was about a motorcycle race—and shook him and said, *You've killed us! We're gonna lose the ballgame.*[3] (Later, when his team went to see *Slap Shot,* the Paul Newman hockey satire, Woody was so incensed by a reference to lesbianism that he shouted, *This is TRASH,* and walked out of the theater.)

He was a small-town guy, a boxer, a naval officer during World War II. He believed the things he believed, and he happened to believe that American society was under siege, that we were becoming submissive and apathetic, that there were people trying to bring down the establishment and the country would not survive if we allowed it to happen. He was paranoid and reactive; because he felt all these things inside, he was, said his former assistant Ara Parseghian, "the most emotional guy I've ever seen, and he got madder than hell at his players. He'd get so emotionally involved and explode. He'd punch kids and yell at them, but off the field he was like a father to them. He was really like two different people."

---

3. According to Jerry Brondfield's *Woody Hayes and the 100-Yard War,* the Buckeyes "won 42–7 or some such." The assistant, however, was relieved of his movie-choosing responsibilities.

For years, Hayes taught a football-coaching class. By all accounts, he was an engaging and patient instructor, and treated many of his own players who took the class in an entirely different way than he treated them on an actual football field.[4] On a football field, Woody Hayes saw himself as a general and a commander. On a football field, he believed, his mission was as serious and as crucial as that of the president. It was his job to control his team, and in so doing, to maintain control over a society that was changing in ways that seemed (to him) frightening and illogical. *Indoctrinate,* Woody once said, was a word "some liberals are against. I am not." This was what a football coach *did*; this was why Woody Hayes believed in football as a counterweight to the hippie protest movement of the '60s, and this was why Woody Hayes was Richard Nixon's favorite coach, and this was why Woody Hayes became the archetype of the Cold War–era football coach.

"People complain that we are victims of a permissive society," he said. "Well, I'll tell you this—we don't have one player on my team who 'does his own thing.'"

VI.

The same year that Ohio State voted to boycott the Rose Bowl, the Big Ten, feeling pressure because of the aggressive recruiting rules

---

4. There is an amazing video of Hayes teaching a "voluntary" vocabulary class to his freshman recruits: He brings up the word *apathy,* tells his players to "avoid it like the plague," and implies that smoking a joint will cause them to do nothing but gaze at their own shoe for an hour.

of the Southeastern Conference, voted to award athletic scholar-
ships irrespective of need or academic performance. Players on
scholarship only needed to maintain a 1.7 grade-point average
their freshman year, a 1.8 as sophomores, a 1.9 as juniors, and a
2.0 as seniors. It was, according to Ohio State student newspaper
the *Lantern,* an ignoble plan, but the other option, of going the
Ivy League route and abolishing athletic scholarships altogether,
would essentially render the Big Ten a second-tier football league.
Facing a crossroads, the Big Ten made the choice to keep up, to
chase the idea that big-time football could become a recruiting
tool for its universities rather than a hindrance. College football
was too ingrained into the culture of the Big Ten to let it go altogether. Ohio State's school president in the early 1950s, Howard
Bevis, often joked that "we should have a university of which the
football team can be proud."[5]

The liberals won the battle. The conservatives, Woody Hayes
foremost among them, won the war.

VII.

The problem was that Woody Hayes could not halt progress.
The problem was that even football could not stand still. And so
Woody Hayes, the Cold War coach, started to become an anach-
ronism. He expressed a firm belief that Richard Nixon was set
up during Watergate. He granted a writer from *Harper's* access to

---

5. Weirdly, some fifty years later, Ohio State president E. Gordon Gee would essentially make the same joke when referring to football coach Jim Tressel.

his program, and when the writer published an unflattering book about his team, Hayes claimed that the writer had been sent by the University of Michigan to destroy him. As offenses opened up to the pass, Woody Hayes buckled down. He did support the civil rights movement, and he proved a moderating influence during student protests of the Vietnam War (a conflict he supported wholeheartedly), but he preferred the 1950s, "when the air was clean and the sex was dirty."

He won his last national championship in 1968, at the height of the protest movement, and the 1970s proved an ugly denouement both for the president and his chosen coach. During the Michigan game in 1971, after storming out onto the field to confront the officials, Woody snapped a yard marker over his knee and tossed it onto the field; at the Rose Bowl after the '72 season, Hayes shoved a *Los Angeles Times* photographer who got too close to him, and was charged with assault (the charges were later dropped). His irascibility had overcome his judgment. The world was closing in. He could no longer restrain the beast inside him.

VIII.

I started following college football, if you can call it that, in 1978, as a five-year-old kid with a preternatural ability to memorize names and jersey numbers. That same fall, during the Gator Bowl, Woody Hayes punched a Clemson player in the throat when they crossed paths on the sideline, ending his career and sealing his reputation as a man who could not overcome his basest instincts. I don't remember if I was watching the Gator Bowl, and even if I was, I doubt I was old enough to have any immediate understanding of what occurred,[6] but there is a part of me, even now, that sympathizes with Woody Hayes. It wasn't the first time Woody had hit a player, and it wasn't even the first time he had slugged an *opposing* player.[7] It was a completely unjustified physical reaction, but this is what football does to us: Other than boxing, it is our culture's most overtly physical mode of expression, which is probably why it feels so paradoxical that it's housed at universities that serve as laboratories of intellectualism.

I mean, I understand what Woody Hayes was trying to do. I understand that he was trying to gain some measure of control over the chaos. I understand that he was deeply involved in the complicated task of both encouraging and moderating violence in young minds. Violence is an essential element of football, and at some level, coaches have to cultivate that urge, in the same way drill sergeants do. It is a fine line, and it can easily be crossed. Hayes was not the first coach who lost his job because he couldn't harness his physicality, and he wasn't the last.[8]

Sometimes you get so angry that you have to let it out. This is why football was invented all those years ago by Ivy League kids looking to blow off steam, and this is why I fell in love with it as an irascible teenager, and this is why it continues to exist even as we recognize that it may slowly be delivering irreversible brain

---

6. Especially since the broadcast crew didn't really address it.

7. He once punched an Iowa player, and according to author Jerry Brondfield, "would have continued with an encore if an Ohio State assistant coach had not leaped onto his back to wrestle him into a semblance of submissiveness."

8. When Rutgers basketball coach Mike Rice was caught on tape verbally and physically abusing his players in 2013, he was widely condemned and eventually fired.

trauma to those who play it. This is why I love to watch it, and this is why it often scares me to death, and this is why I sometimes feel ashamed that I love it as much as I do. This is why I often think Woody Hayes was an anachronistic bully for his actions, and this is why I often think Woody Hayes was a genius for recognizing that his methods were a necessary motivator.

There is a thing that happens to me when I'm watching certain college football games, and it is driven by a feeling I cannot explain. I didn't even know what it looked like until my best friend, and then my wife, pointed it out to me: They told me I became so intense that it frightened them a little. My wife had to leave the room. It was, they said, as if they could no longer recognize me; it was, they said, almost like I became another person. I don't know if I've grown up to become an irascible man, but in those moments, I become an irascible child all over again. In those moments, I lose control, and I let go, and just as I imagine it was for Woody Hayes, it feels like a kind of relief.

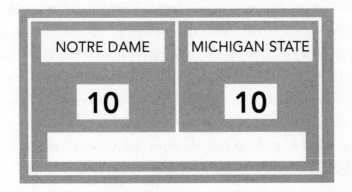

NOTRE DAME   MICHIGAN STATE

10   10

November 11, 1966

Kissing Your Sister

Discussion Topics: Ara Parseghian • "Games of the Century" • The Polls • The Argument • The Minnesota Golden Gophers • George Wallace • KILL BUBBA KILL • Anticlimaxes

I.

So let us imagine you are a college football coach in a hypothetical universe, and your team is ranked No. 1 in the country, and you are playing the No. 2 team on their home field, late in the season. The game is tied, and you have the ball with a minute and a half to play at roughly your own thirty-yard line. Do you sit on the ball and play for overtime, or do you throw underneath, and run the hurry-up, mix in a draw or two, and utilize your time-outs?

The answer, unless your hypothetical universe relies heavily on the triple option, is almost certainly the latter. The answer is to go aggressive, because in the twenty-first century, ninety seconds with even a marginally competent quarterback is a virtual eternity, and because, if you have recruited a decent kicker and not drafted some long-haired punk off the hypothetical soccer team at this hypothetical slacker liberal-arts college of yours, you only need to pick up roughly thirty-five to forty yards against what will almost certainly be a soft prevent defense in order to have a shot at a game-winning field goal. This is college football today: In 2012, Alabama trailed LSU 17–14 when they got the ball back with 1:34 left in the fourth quarter. The Crimson Tide had to rely on a struggling quarterback in a run-heavy offense, going against one of the best defenses in the country, with the ball at their own twenty-eight; they scored the winning touchdown in forty-three seconds. They scored so quickly it almost felt like they did it *too fast*.

And this is the problem Ara Parseghian has faced for the past fifty years, in defending the most impactful occupational decision of his career: Modernity has only made it look worse.

II.

So now let us imagine it is a different era, and two-platoon football—the idea that separate groups of players should compete on offense and defense—is in its infancy, and there is no such thing as overtime, and your university does not yet accept bowl bids, and anyway, the polls only take into account regular-season games. Your starting quarterback has been flattened by a six-foot-six, 280-pound lineman named Bubba who will some-day become known for his roles as the brick shithouse of a cop in a series of Steve Guttenberg films about inept police recruits; your backup is a nineteen-year-old recently diagnosed diabetic who appears to have shed most of his stamina and is overthrow-ing receivers by several feet. Your kicker has attempted four field goals all season, and while he has made three of them, he missed from forty-one yards earlier in the quarter; besides, it is the era of straight-ahead kicking, and field goals are a far more dicey proposition.

You are undefeated and ranked No. 1, and your opponent is undefeated and ranked No. 2, and this contest is tied at 10–10, and you have one game left to play and your opponent has none. There is one other undefeated team, but you have the advantage over that team, because that team is ranked third. You recognize that if you choose to burn out those last ninety seconds, and then you dispatch a decent-but-not-great Southern California team, you will retain the favor of the pollsters, in large part because you are *not* the head coach of some hypothetical university: You are the head coach of the Notre Dame Fighting Irish, who represent the hypothetical university that millions of urban commuters like to act as if they attended.

Let us imagine that you are Ara Parseghian, and it is 1966, and you are involved in yet another iteration of the Game of the Century, perhaps the Gamiest of Them All. Knowing that you may very well win a national championship by doing nothing, do you still choose risk?

III.

There have been multiple "Games of the Century" since Michigan State and Notre Dame so emphatically defied resolution: at least six more in the latter half of the twentieth century, and two more in the twenty-first, not to mention the dozens more that morphed into Games of the Century after the fact, rather than through the Barnumesque pregame hoopla fueled by newspapers and wire services and television networks and college marketing departments. In fact, no sport has repeatedly co-opted the term "Game of the Century" like college football.[1] It's not even close. And the reason for this is obvious: In other major American sports, there is a championship game (or series, or playoff bracket), and that championship game (or series, or playoff bracket) is *already* considered, by default, the potential Game of the Century. There is a *Super* Bowl. There is a *World* Series. There is March *Madness* and an NBA *Finals*—a word that signifies a clear-cut ending. The hype is built into the postseason system.

But this is not true in college football.

This is not true in college football because for nearly all of its existence, it has sought to exist outside the realm of virtually every other major American sport. This is not true in college football because the sport has clung to the incongruous notion of marrying amateurism with big business, and in order to preserve this conception, and satisfy their business interests, the powers-that-be have shied away from any sort of definitive postseason format. It makes some sense:

---

1. In that time, there has been one soccer Game of the Century, one college basketball game, one chess match, and one iteration of the Japanese board game Go.

To admit that there *should* be an unambiguous No. 1 would be to admit that the concept of who's No. 1 matters in the first place, which would defy the rickety foundation upon which the sport was built.

And so there is no weirder and more contentious histori-cal annex than that of college football, during the roughly 145 years of what I guess will come to be known as the "pre-playoff era." There are all sorts of schools who take credit for all sorts of national championships to which they have only specious claims[2]; on top of that, all of the so-called Games of the Century have taken place during the regular season rather than the bowl season. Two of them ended in ties. For all that hype, for all those tickets sold above resale value, for all those television eyes . . . at the end of the season, when it came to determining who the national champion might be, the majority of college football's greatest games have actually served to resolve nothing at all.

IV.

We should head back to the 1920s for a moment, because before then, the concept of a "national championship" essentially did

---

2. Exhibit A: Alabama, which asserts its right to national championships in, A) 1973, despite losing to Notre Dame in the Sugar Bowl; B) 1941, despite a two-loss season that saw them finish twentieth in the Associated Press poll; and C) 1964, despite a loss to Texas in the Orange Bowl, because the AP did not issue a post-bowl-games poll. (The Crimson Tide reversed that logic in 1965, laying claim to a national championship despite finishing fourth in the final regular season coaches' poll.) But it's not just the Tide who have taken the liberty to manipulate history: Cornell lays claim to the 1923 national championship, despite the fact that the gen-eral consensus was with either Illinois or Michigan. And Princeton claims the 1869 title, even though Rutgers and Princeton split the only two games played.

not exist. And maybe, in retrospect, this was the happiest time for college football, since it trafficked mostly in blissful ignorance. (In 1923, ten teams went undefeated and untied, and at least four could have made a legitimate claim toward a national title, if only they had the means back then.) "Nobody argued about it, preoccupied as most people were with striking for an eight-hour workday," Dan Jenkins wrote in his book *Saturday's America*. "Nobody even cared. You told a friend that your school was No. 1 in those days and all he said was, 'Listen, that's great. But excuse me, I've got to go invent the airplane.'"

The question wasn't even a question until we made it one: Up to then, this was a regional pastime, invented on a muddy New Jersey pitch, imported southward and westward, delineated into conferences whose members clawed over trophies shaped like water jugs and cutting implements and bronzed swine. And, with the exception of a few rogue magazine writers declaring "mythical national champions," this was enough.

This was enough, because no one conceived of anything more, because professional sports and television had not shaped us into creatures in need of concrete resolution. This was enough, because America seemingly had more important concerns, like jazz and women's suffrage and institutional bribery and stock market bubbles. Which brings us to a classroom at the University of Illinois, and to an economics instructor named Frank G. Dickinson, who had, as a hobby, developed a mathematical system to rate all of the college football teams in America.

Dickinson's system was crude and unrefined: It afforded a team more points for a win over a "first-division" squad—which, if I may get technical for a second, referred to a team that won more games than it lost—and it split points for ties, and it sometimes produced results that seem retrospectively stupid. But Dickinson spoke about his system on campus one day, and the *Daily Illini* reported on this speech, and this caught the eye of a Chicago clothier named Jack Rissman, who wished to sponsor a trophy delivered to the champion of what was then the Big Nine Conference, in those bygone days when the Big Ten actually lacked a surfeit of member institutions.

And hereupon we stumble across the first deliberate corruption of what I call, for lack of a better term, The Argument: Hearing about Dickinson's system, Knute Rockne invited the professor and the clothier to South Bend, and asked if perhaps they might consider making their trophy a national trophy, so that Notre Dame could be eligible to win it. *And while you're at it,* Rockne said, *how about you predate the system by four years or so, and make the 1924 Irish with the "Four Horsemen" the first official national champions?*

Frank Dickinson obliged. The Four Horsemen were retroactively elevated into myth. His ratings—which, like most in the early history of college football polling, did not consider postseason games—became the first of the gospels, and he was joined by a host of imitators and pretenders to the throne. There was Deke Houlgate—whose system, Jenkins wrote, "so far as anyone could tell, was his personal opinion"[3]—and there was William F. Boand, who sought to combine the best aspects of the Dickinson system along with those of a couple of other uni-

---

3. That's not entirely true: According to a website run by Houlgate's grandson, the Houlgate system is formulated through *letter grades* that were essentially based on Houlgate's personal opinion.

versity professors into something called the Azzi Ratem system. There was Dick Dunkel and his power index, and Paul Williamson and his power ratings, and Frank Litkenhous and his "difference by score" system. There was Parke H. Davis, the football historian, who in the mid-1930s chose the national champion for every season to date according to his own whims.[4] And then finally, along came the Associated Press, led by sports editor Alan Gould.

In 1936, the first year of the Associated Press poll, there were at least sixteen different national championship surveys: Seven (including the AP) chose Minnesota (even though the Gophers lost to Northwestern), five chose Pittsburgh (even though the Panthers lost to Duquesne and tied Fordham), one chose Duke (which lost to Tennessee), one picked LSU (which tied Texas and lost to Santa Clara), and one picked Alabama (which tied Tennessee). (The sixteenth pollster, Grantland Rice, chose Yale, which lost to Dartmouth but had a coach named Ducky Pond, and we all know Granny Rice—who originated the overwrought moniker for Notre Dame's Four Horsemen, among others—couldn't resist a good nickname.)

"It was a case of thinking up ideas to develop interest and controversy," Gould said years later, explaining the origin of the AP poll. "Papers wanted materials to fill space between games. That's all I had in mind, something to keep the pot boiling. Sports then was living off controversy, opinion, whatever. This was just another exercise in hoopla."

---

4. Weirdly, Davis, in reexamining at the 1924 Four Horsemen season, chose 9-1-1 Penn over undefeated Notre Dame.

Dickinson ceased his polling in 1940. Soon enough, the Associated Press poll, born out of hype and based on nothing more than intuition and whimsy, became the standings of record.

V.

There has never been (and never will be) a more fascinating and socially fraught iteration of college football's perpetual popularity contest than in 1966. The preseason No. 1 in the Associated Press poll was all-white Alabama, and the Crimson Tide went 11-0 and finished third in the final standings; the No. 1 team for the early part of the regular season was Michigan State, the first contender ever with more black starters than white, which went 10-0-1, finished second in the final poll behind the team it had tied, and could not play in the Rose Bowl anyway because they had done so the year before[5]; and the No. 1 team for the latter half of the season was (almost entirely white) Notre Dame, which had not yet deemed itself plebian enough to accept a bowl bid, and clung to that No. 1 ranking in all of the major indices, the AP poll and the coaches' poll and the Football Writers Association of America poll, at season's end.

There is a legitimate case to be made for all three teams, and there is a legitimate case to be made against all three, and looming

---

5. The Big Ten, which struggled to reconcile the overtly commercial nature of bowl games like the Rose with the member schools' academic mission, clung to this arcane socialistic bylaw until 1971. In addition, Big Ten teams were yoked exclusively to the Rose Bowl until the mid-1970s, meaning if they didn't qualify, they couldn't play in any other bowl game, either.

over everything is politics—both the microcosmal politics of college football itself and the overwhelming racial politics of the era, so much of which was centered on college campuses. When you choose your champions through popular opinion polls, the real world is bound to creep in.

Earlier that same year, an all-black Texas Western team defeated an all-white Kentucky team in the NCAA basketball national championship game. It was a stark and straightforward affirmation of the civil rights movement, and no one could accuse Texas Western of being undeserving. But college football had no such definitive system for determining a champion. College football would take another thirty years just to settle on an equitable way to break ties. Which is why there are those who still believe that a segregationist governor had as much to do with determining the national champion in 1966 as Ara Parseghian ever did.

VI.

I'm not merely paraphrasing a Drive-By Truckers song[6] here: This is the conventional wisdom about 1966 from those Alabama fans who still recall it. Author Keith Dunnavant's book *The Missing Ring,* which focuses entirely on the perceived injustice of Ala-

---

6. The Truckers, a seminal southern alt-rock band of the '00s, did have a spoken-word song called "Three Great Alabama Icons," which is about Bear Bryant, George Wallace, and Ronnie Van Zant of Lynyrd Skynyrd. In it, singer Patterson Hood mentions Bryant's "red checkered hat," which was actually black-and-white houndstooth, but it's still an insightful seven-minute breakdown of Alabama's fraught political climate in the 1970s, from a dude who admittedly was not a football fan but drank a lot of malt liquor.

bama's 1966 season,[7] states: "Given the chance, Alabama could have beaten Notre Dame, Michigan State, or any of the other contenders for the title. But the Crimson Tide was no match for George Wallace and all he represented."

That first sentence is nothing but hyperbolic speculation by Dunnavant, who also wrote a Bear Bryant biography and tends to get a little carried away with his advocacy. It's in the second sentence where things get complicated, and it's in the second sentence that we exhume the tensions of the civil rights era in the South, and the spectre of Wallace, the only person in Alabama whose stature compared with that of Bryant. And so it's in reading that second sentence that you find yourself faced with a critical question: Namely, what are the parameters of The Argument? Should it matter that Alabama was an all-white team in a state where the governor was perhaps the nation's most outspoken segregationist? If voting against Alabama might even potentially hasten the reversal of a grave injustice, should this be considered?

Or should the games themselves be the only things that matter?

VII.

Bear Bryant confessed a special fondness for his 1966 team, and I'm sure this is partly because he felt they were treated unfairly by the national media, but I imagine it is also because Bryant recognized the headwind he was facing; as the 1960s carried toward

---

7. Subtitle: *How Bear Bryant and the 1966 Alabama Crimson Tide Were Denied College Football's Most Elusive Prize.*

their inevitable conclusion, he came to realize that he could no longer win with (in his own words) "skinny white boys." Not that he wanted to persist in trying: History has shown that Bryant was barbarous in his methods,[8] but not in his philosophy. He tried to integrate his teams at Kentucky and Texas A&M, and if not for the overarching political stamp of George Wallace, he may have integrated his Crimson Tide teams far sooner than he did. He had already won national championships in 1964 and 1965,[9] and the 1966 squad was the last of his great all-white squads: The Tide would not win another Southeastern Conference title until after they had black players on scholarship.

You watch highlights of that '66 Alabama team, and it's hard to discern the tackles from the backs. I imagine there are fifth-grade teams in Texas with more bulk today. Only one of their offensive linemen weighed more than two hundred pounds; when Bryant recruited a six-foot-six, 280-pound lineman out of Louisville, he immediately put him on a crash diet and asked him to lose fifty pounds. He despised "fat bellies," according to Dunnavant, and succeeded with blocking schemes that utilized angularity and quickness. But as their rivals swelled in size, this only contributed to the perception that Alabama—as a football program, as a university, as a state—was clinging

---

8. Bryant's famously torturous summer camp in Junction, Texas—no water breaks in 100-degree heat—would get him summarily fired and blackballed in modern America, and possibly brought up on criminal charges. But, because it happened in 1954, they just made a TV movie about it.

9. You could make the case that Alabama was undeserving in either of those previous seasons, but especially in 1964, when the Crimson Tide lost to Texas in the Orange Bowl and No. 2 Arkansas defeated Nebraska in the Cotton Bowl. Of course, bowls weren't factored into the national championship picture back then, but this does not stop Alabama fans from affirming that their (equally meaningless) thrashing of Nebraska in the Sugar Bowl two years later validates their claim to the '66 title.

stubbornly to outmoded (and overtly racist) values. That November, a few weeks before Notre Dame played Michigan State, George Wallace (who had served out his term limit) managed to get his wife, Lurleen, elected governor, thereby reendorsing Alabama's segregationist policies.

And all of this gave the voters—especially those voters in the Northeast and Midwest, in media hubs like New York City and Chicago—an excuse to demote the Crimson Tide: Before they'd even played a game, they dropped from first to third in the polls. They were smaller, and whiter, and from a visual perspective, at least, they could no longer compare.

"[I]f Bryant and Alabama had at least attempted to integrate the team just three years earlier," wrote author (and Bryant biographer) Allen Barra, "Alabama would almost certainly have been national champs in 1966."

VIII.

The team that took their place at No. 1 may have been just as apt a representative of the South: Of Michigan State's seventeen black players, ten were from below the Mason-Dixon Line. Twelve of their twenty-two starters were black, including their quarterback, Jimmy Raye; eight of their defensive starters were black, including Bubba Smith of Beaumont, Texas, who was six-foot-eight, and 285 pounds, wore size-52 extra-long suits, and was fast enough to do his sprints with the backs.[10]

---

10. Said Michigan State's track coach, according to Mike Celizic's *The Biggest Game of Them All:* "I'd like to have Bubba on the track team, but he's too big to run in one lane."

Smith was the son of a draconian high school football coach who once gave each of his players a public lashing with a leather belt when they were trailing at halftime. He wanted to follow his brother to Kansas, but they didn't want another Smith there; he wanted to go to the University of Texas, but like most other southern schools in the early 1960s, they couldn't take him. And so he went to East Lansing, having never really interacted with white society before. The first time he unfolded his frame from the bed and stood up to meet his white roommate, the roommate's parents nearly fainted.[11] It was not a utopian community—Smith and his teammates often had trouble finding an apartment to rent in town—but Bubba had an unmistakable charm. (KILL BUBBA KILL, his fellow students chanted at him.) He reportedly joined a Jewish fraternity; he was voted the most popular student on campus, even as he tested the limits of authority. His senior year, he drove an Oldsmobile with his name written in gold letters on the door, most likely paid for through the largesse of alumni and boosters. Occasionally, Bubba parked it in the university president's space.[12]

---

11. "But [the parents] didn't leave," Celizic wrote. "Bubba didn't have an attitude about anything."

12. If all this sounds like a movie, that's because it sort of was. Smith later played a similar character onscreen, a lovable giant who was never quite as manipulable as he let on. He made a few Miller Lite commercials that played off tortured football metaphors, but once he realized that he'd become more closely associated with the culture of drinking than with the game he played, he stopped doing them. He went into acting at a time when the possibilities for an eighty-inch-tall mustachioed black man were limited to novelty cameos, and he won enough respect to become a series regular on a couple of short-lived programs. It would be a stretch to say that Smith was a brilliant actor, but he was always genuine. There is no way, even now, to make an unironic defense of the *Police Academy* movies, but Smith was the realest thing about them. He could not mimic police sirens with his vocal cords, and he did not fall into comic tantrums, and he wasn't a cheeky, hipster dickhead like Steve Guttenberg's character. He didn't really say much at all; mostly, he spoke with his physicality, with a blend of intimidation and charm, and he won over a generation of suburban white kids without sacrificing his dignity.

No other major college program had ever been this black, and such diversity was fostered by Michigan State's gregarious head coach, Duffy Daugherty, who scoured the Pacific and the South and even went to Hawaii to find recruits. There were times Bear Bryant (along with other southern coaches) directed black athletes he couldn't recruit himself into Daugherty's hands.

The Spartans won their first four games that season, and then they slogged to an 11–8 win over a middling Ohio State team in the mud and rain. When Notre Dame beat North Carolina 32–0 that same week, the Irish leapt to No. 1. It surprised no one. Wrote author Mike Celizic: "It was a fact of life that Notre Dame was the darling of the media in New York, the media capital of the nation"—a fact that dated back to the Knute Rockne era—"and was also almost the home team in Chicago."

In any other sport, this inherent advantage wouldn't mean anything. The size of Kentucky's fan base could not aid them against Texas Western, but in college football in 1966, when the media had full control of the most impactful of all the polls, it afforded Ara Parseghian a distinct political advantage. Since Michigan State and Notre Dame were scheduled to meet in late November, it appeared that this advantage would be rendered moot. Somebody would win, and somebody would lose.

But instead, nothing happened.

IX.

If you want to trace the moment when the NCAA began to lose control of its product, you could probably begin by pinpointing this particular Game of the Century. Until that Saturday, the television networks had shown one game each week, and each team could only appear once on national TV each season. That policy emerged largely because of Notre Dame: The Irish and the University of Pennsylvania had both aired all their home games in 1950,[13] and fearing a decline in attendance, the NCAA acted in self-defense and regulated the national schedule. And now, a decade later, facing widespread protest that the Notre Dame–Michigan State game would only be aired in certain regions—more than twenty thousand people signed a petition, and one man in a blacked-out area filed a lawsuit claiming his constitutional rights were being violated[14]—ABC agreed to air it nationally on a two-hour tape delay. (Even then, a Miami attorney named Dan Ginsberg flew to New York just so he could watch it live.[15])

"Notre Dame was the biggest thing in college football," said ABC's Chris Schenkel, who did the play-by-play for the broadcast, "and while that might not have mattered on the field, the mystique of Notre Dame was a big force off the field."

X.

In some ways, I sympathize with Ara Parseghian. He is, by all accounts, a decent and intelligent man who (even deep into his

---

13. Penn sold the rights to its home games to ABC for $150,000, and Notre Dame sold theirs to the DuMont network—which was, at that point, slightly larger than ABC—for $185,000.

14. The suit was thrown out.

15. According to Celizic's book, Ginsberg spent more than $150 for a hotel room and a plane ticket so he could avoid waiting those extra two hours.

retirement)[16] has been forced to repeatedly defend a decision that was pragmatically correct: For years, until the tiebreaking rules were changed in the mid-1990s, Parseghian's name would arise during a television broadcast whenever a coach faced up to the political and strategic question of playing for a tie. He'd come to Notre Dame in 1964 and revived it from a moribund period,[17] and he'd become so instantly popular, so deeply tied in to Notre Dame's faith-based ethos, that during a winter storm amid the final home game of his first season, the students chanted, "Ara, Stop the Snow!" In many ways, head football coach at Notre Dame is a political position, and Ara managed the politics as well as anybody, and you cannot blame him or his university for taking advantage of the stature the job afforded him.

That's all he did in the final ninety seconds of the Game of the Century, by choosing to sit on the ball. He'd lost his starting center to injury; his quarterback, Coley O'Brien, was not right, most likely because his diabetes had caught up to him; he actually *did* go for it on a fourth-and-short with time running out, just to prevent Michigan State from kicking a last-second field goal. And Duffy Daugherty, facing a fourth-and-four at his own thirty-six, had chosen to punt back to Notre Dame on the Spartans' last drive, knowing full well that he might not get the ball back, and knowing full well that Notre Dame had an inherent polling advantage.

So maybe we lay too much blame on Ara. Maybe all Ara did

---

16. As I write this, Parseghian is fast approaching his ninety-first birthday.

17. The previous two coaches, Joe Kuharich and Hugh Devore, had won nineteen games and lost thirty between 1959 and 1963.

was recognize the contours of The Argument. Maybe all he did was conform to the system, the way a good coach should.

With the score tied at 10, and Notre Dame—which had one black player on its roster, All-American Alan Page—bleeding out the clock, Bubba Smith said to his teammates, "If this game ends in a tie, Notre Dame is going to win. All the sportswriters are Catholic."

And then he said, "Do you think we're going to win the national championship even if they run the clock out? We got too many niggers on this team to win the national championship. We have to find a way."

Smith admitted he said these things to exhort his teammates, but he also said them because he believed these things to be true. He believed that Ara Parseghian did the right thing for himself— in part because he is certain the Irish couldn't have moved the ball against Michigan State's defense on that final drive, but mostly because Parseghian read the politics correctly, because he crafted an explanation that was both plausible to his supporters and infuriating to his detractors. It is the same explanation Ara uses all these years later.

"We didn't go for a tie," he said in 2012. "The game *ended* in a tie."

XI.

And it's quotes like these that explain why Ara's decision, right or wrong, aroused so much emotion: Because he sold it as if it were guided by forces outside of his control. Because it felt passive, and passivity cut against the grain in this sport. BAMA PLAYS FOOTBALL; N. DAME PLAYS POLITICS,[18] read one sign at the Orange Bowl, which Alabama won 34–7 over Nebraska. (Notre Dame, following its 51–0 win over the University of Southern California, stayed home for the bowl season: From 1924 until 1969, the Irish didn't play in a single bowl game, considering them an unnecessary adornment to the season.)

In football, you do not settle; in football, you do not back down. In football you gamble, and if Ara was inherently not the gambler that Duffy Daugherty was,[19] then maybe he deserved the criticism he got for backing into a national title rather than attempting to take it by force. Dan Jenkins mocked Ara's choice in *Sports Illustrated*—"Old Notre Dame will tie over all," was the lead, a play on the Notre Dame fight song—setting the historical tone for decades to come.[20] In his book about the '66 Alabama team, Dunnavant launches into a weirdly ideological rant, labeling Ara's act "rebellious and utterly antiestablishment," comparing him to bra burners and war protesters and acid heads, noting, "It was like seeing John Wayne parade around the room in high heels and a strapless gown." Bryant himself, acknowledging that some of his players would soon be sent off to Vietnam, said, "I hope they aren't going over there for a tie."

---

18. The irony being that, by fielding an all-white team, Bryant was also conforming to political will.

19. Both literally and metaphorically, since Daugherty was apparently no stranger to the racetrack: "The only place where windows clean people," he said, after spending a day at Santa Anita.

20. Well, at least for those who recognized Notre Dame's lobbying power was impacting the very nature of the sport: In South Bend, they actually burned copies of *SI*.

"I don't think any other school would have won the champi-onship if they had done that," Bubba Smith said.

And so you had an all-white team complaining that they'd been shut out due to political concerns, and a majority black team complaining that they'd been shut out for the same reasons. And all of this fury began to drive, for the first time, a real argument about the nature of The Argument itself.

Soon afterward, Duffy Daugherty floated the possibility of an eight-team playoff; the idea went to a committee, where, like every other anti-Argument possibility floated for the next forty-five years, it died a slow and silent death. People were angry at what Ara didn't do, but even more so, they began to recognize that the system itself had not adapted to modernity—that maybe The Argument could not be conducted fairly if everyone came at it with their own biases.

Of course, what Ara did was not driven by antiestablishment thought; it was driven by just the opposite. What he did appealed *directly* to the establishment, which at that point happened to consist of that rarefied group of people who voted in college foot-ball polls. Notre Dame finished first in every poll that mattered in 1966. By playing to his base, Ara won the election.

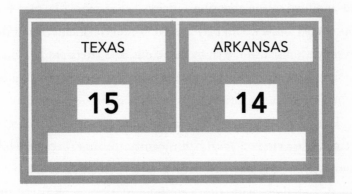

TEXAS	ARKANSAS
15	14

December 6, 1969

Does Your Conscience Bother You?

Discussion Topics: Richard Nixon • Darrell Royal • Southern Football • Regional/Racial Politics • Player Revolt • Coaches' Paranoia • "Pooch Kick Frank" • The Early Iconography of Joe Paterno • Rattlesnakes

I.

On the first Friday of December 1969, as Walter Cronkite prepared to report on the emerging details of the My Lai Massacre and on the occupation by black students of the Harvard administration building, White House press secretary Ron Ziegler held an odd and frenetic briefing that played out like a screwball political satire. That morning, the questioning veered into the fraught and partisan regionalism of college football, and to Richard Nixon's self-anointed role in choosing a national champion: The next day, top-ranked Texas would play at second-ranked Arkansas, and the president himself would sit in the stands, and afterward he would present the winner with a plaque declaring this team the unquestioned No. 1 in the land.

This whole plaque thing was Nixon's call, and I'm sure it seemed like a clever tactical brainstorm at the time, because while many southerners had cast their vote for Nixon in 1968, many others had sided with the segregationist George Wallace; and because an October article in the *New York Times* headlined, "In the South, Football is a Religio-Social Pastime"—which, I suppose, still qualified as news back then—had been making the rounds among the White House staff. This was college football's centennial season, and the Texas-Arkansas game was its marquee matchup (which had been moved to the final week of the regular season, largely through the efforts and foresight of a shrewd ABC television executive named Beano Cook).[1]

By sitting in the stands, as Nixon often did at sporting events, he could present himself as a "regular guy," and by serving as the arbiter of college football's perpetual Argument, Nixon could elevate himself into a declarative authority on the sport. And in so doing, he could cravenly appeal directly to a

---

1. "ABC came out looking smarter than a treeful of owls," Texas coach Darrell Royal told Terry Frei in Frei's book *Horns, Hogs, and Nixon Coming*, and that is exactly the kind of thing I imagine Darrell Royal will say if I ever meet him in the afterlife. (Beano Cook went on to become an eccentric television raconteur up until his death in 2012. He once predicted that a Notre Dame quarterback named Ron Powlus would win two Heisman Trophies before he'd played a single college game, a prophecy that came up two Heismans short.)

pair of southern states[2] that figured into his overarching electoral stratagem.

Of course, it wasn't *entirely* craven, since Richard Nixon really
did like college football, probably more than he liked southerners.
A few weeks earlier, he'd marked the occasion of a 250,000-person
anti–Vietnam War rally outside his home by staying indoors and
watching Ohio State beat Purdue by four touchdowns.[3] So a college football game seemed like a good look for a man who often
appeared out of his element around people of any kind.

II.

Hence, the following memo, from staffer Harry Dent to chief of
staff H. R. Haldeman and appointments secretary Dwight Chapin:

October 6, 1969

FOR: Dwight Chapin
       Bob Haldeman
FROM: Harry S. Dent

If at any time during the remainder of this term the president wants to see and be seen by a tremendous crowd of
enthusiastic Southerners, I suggest we consider sending him
to one of the big football rivalry games.

---

2. Nixon lost Texas in 1968 by fewer than 40,000 votes to Hubert Humphrey,
while George Wallace garnered more than half a million votes in the state; Wallace
won Arkansas by about 46,000 votes over Nixon.

3. Nixon was once described as a "fearless, if ineffectual" player while warming the
bench at Whittier College.

The attached article from the *New York Times* points out very truly that football is a religio-social pastime in the South, particularly when you get teams like Alabama and Mississippi playing. That would be a good way to get him into a key Southern state and get to see many good people from two states, without doing anything political.

"We expect our presidents to be one of us, and we expect them to be above us somehow," says Nicholas Evan Sarantakes, a historian at the U.S. Naval War College who wrote a yet-to-be published book on Nixon and sports (and who forwarded me a copy of the memo). "This was an effort to hit both of those things."

What amazes me, all these years later, is not the blatant electoral calculus of this gesture. What amazes me is that Richard Nixon, who so adored this sport that it was one of the few things he could talk fluently about with his ideological opponents (including, most famously, Hunter S. Thompson)—and who actually spoke of an alternate existence in which he became a sportswriter—did not anticipate the implications of getting personally involved in the declaration of a national champion, as sportswriters had been doing with a lack of definitive success for decades. What amazes me is that a man as shrewd as Nixon, who surely must have been paying attention to the Notre Dame–Michigan State–Alabama fracas of 1966, did not foresee the partisan political thicket he'd wandered into.

How could Richard Nixon, of all people, not comprehend that when it came to choosing a mythical national champion, the president of the United States had no real gravitas at all? That, in the end, in a situation like this, the truth was nothing but a matter of geographical perspective?

At that Friday press briefing, Ziegler was confronted about the complaints of Raymond Shafer, the Republican governor of Pennsylvania, expressed in a telegram sent to the White House and in Shafer's own grandstanding press conference that same day championing the merits of Penn State; he was queried, further, about the championship viability of undefeated (and third-ranked) Penn State, coached by an outspoken Brooklyn-born Republican named Joe Paterno.[4]

Ziegler responded by saying he was certain that the winner of the Texas-Arkansas game deserved the national championship, and then, realizing that this was an unsatisfactory response on both political fronts, he sprinted back to the Oval Office, huddled with the president, and upon his return to the briefing room said his boss was considering an "appropriate" gesture if Penn State also finished undefeated. A reporter asked, "What sort of gesture?" and Ziegler retreated to the Oval Office again, and returned shortly afterward, and said Penn State, which had not lost in twenty-nine straight games, would be rewarded with a plaque honoring them for having the longest unbeaten streak of any major college team in the nation.

Now it was getting farcical. This was clearly not an amenable solution, either in the short term or the long term; ninety thousand letters and telegrams had come pouring in from Pennsylvania, and a few Penn State alums actually picketed the White

---

4. Nixon had lost Pennsylvania by fewer than two hundred thousand votes to Hubert Humphrey in 1968; without Wallace on the ballot, he might have won it.

House.[5] But hell, Ron Ziegler was running two hours late for a lunch, and when a reporter brought up the possibility of Texas and Arkansas playing a tie game, as Notre Dame and Michigan State had done in 1966, and then asked, *Wouldn't Nixon be rewarding the wrong plaque to the wrong team?* . . .

"Gentlemen," Ziegler said. "I've done all I can."

Someone else asked if the president was sorry he'd gotten involved in the national championship fracas in the first place. But the press secretary did not answer the question. By then, Ron Ziegler had left the room for the last time that day.

III.

That week in Fayetteville, Arkansas, a black student protesting the band's playing of "Dixie" was shot in the leg by an unknown assailant on campus; a group of black students considered lying down on the field at halftime if the band did decide to go ahead and play "Dixie." Vietnam protesters gathered on a hill near the stadium and displayed a peace sign made of crosses during the game. None of this made the national news at the time—in his accounts of Texas's 15–14 win in his book *Saturday's America,* Dan Jenkins does not mention these peripheral occurrences, choosing instead to focus on partisan zealotry, as in a church marquee displaying a pro-Hogs message. And yet taken together, all of it helps explain why southern college football took on a symbolic political

---

5. "We looked it up," one of the protesters said, "and found he has no such powers in the Constitution."

importance to Nixon in 1969: because everyone involved seemed to recognize that this game, with nary an African-American player on either roster, was the last of its kind.

You could feel the college game shifting underfoot by then, because what better proxy was there of the authoritarian state than a sport that demanded fealty to a dictatorial figure? In the Northeast, in the West, in the Midwest, this very notion was being challenged. At Oregon State, black players protested after a linebacker was suspended for refusing to shave his (well-trimmed) beard and mustache. At Maryland, coach Bob Ward resigned after slapping several players during an off-season workout, prompting alumni, parents, and administrators to berate the school's athletic director for "let[ting] the hippies overthrow the coach." At Wyoming, fourteen black players who asked to wear armbands during a home game against BYU in order to protest the Mormon church's policies were suspended and kicked off the team, both because they weren't allowed to participate in political activities of any kind, and because no "group actions" were allowed by coach Lloyd Eaton, who told them they had the option of "go[ing] back to picking cotton." At Washington, four black players were suspended for a lack of dedication to the program, and at Indiana, sixteen black players were suspended for boycotting a practice. Amid all this, *Sports Illustrated*'s John Underwood ran an alarmist three-part series titled "The Desperate Coach," about the moral and ethical challenges college coaches were dealing with (although as author Michael Oriard pointed out, Underwood did not quote a single player in any of the articles).

"Don't they know what it takes to win?" Ward, the Maryland coach, had told Underwood, who ascribed much of the unrest to radical organizations like Students for a Democratic Society. Bear Bryant at Alabama explained that the solution, for the embattled coach, was "an ironclad contract to protect him against his superiors."

And this explained the appeal of southern football to Nixon, and this explained the appeal of southern football to its white denizens: Even in '69, at the height of everything that would come to define the era, football in places like Tuscaloosa and Fayetteville stood apart from it all. Football in the South was the last vestige of the old America, and the coaches reflected that.

"I don't know anybody who wasn't scared to death [of him]," one Texas player said of Darrell Royal, his coach in '69.

Other than Bryant, Royal was perhaps the most authoritarian coach of them all. He would soon have an unflattering book (titled *Meat on the Hoof*) written about him by a former player, but at this moment, with his Longhorns undefeated, his authority went unquestioned. You did not hang out in Coach Royal's office and shoot the bull with him: "That would be like me going to play with rattlesnakes," one player said. If he suggested that you needed to cut your damn hair, you cut your damn hair. There is a scene in Terry Frei's book *Horns, Hogs, and Nixon Coming* where Royal—driving an orange Cadillac convertible—confronts a drunken player after he is arrested for pulling up onto a curb in the middle of the night. *You can't go through life this way,* he says. *STRAIGHTEN YOURSELF OUT! You only get so many chances in life, son, and you're running out of them.* The player, Frei writes, was "scared sober."

(As I read that, I found myself flashing forward, to the eve of the American bicentennial, to a time when the old ways had passed, to a moment when a fictional Texas football coach delivers essentially the same speech in Richard Linklater's *Dazed and Confused,* and his quarterback responds by partying all night long at the moon tower.)

Fayetteville was not there yet. I imagine if you polled the crowd that day in Fayetteville, they would have been overwhelmingly pro–George Wallace, and they would have stood firmly against the notion that blacks should have any role at all in the sport that had become a socioreligious pastime. "A football weekend when two big Southern schools clash is largely an all-white event," read the October *Times* article that so enamored the White House staff. But then, this is pretty much the unsubtle subtext of Harry Dent's memo. It is remarkable how two paragraphs that end with the words "without doing anything political" can be so rampantly political: *Here is a way to appeal to the white voters we may need in '72.*

"They were the last of how it was," Frei writes of the '69 Longhorns, and I suppose, to Richard Nixon, this was what mattered. Even if he rewarded the wrong plaque to the wrong team, he'd still be appealing to the right people.

IV.

Presidents entangle themselves with sports to political ends all the time, but never had there been such a direct and unambiguous declaration from a chief executive as what Nixon had inserted himself into in '69. Any real opportunity Penn State had to capture the national championship, beyond a Texas loss in the bowl game, had essentially been quashed.

With Penn State, it was, as always, a matter of perception: One hundred years after its origin on a thatch of New Jersey mud, and some fifty years since the hegemony of the Ivy League had been broken, eastern college football was considered weak and inferior, and the Nittany Lions' unbeaten streak seen by many as nothing more than an intriguing footnote to the national conversation. The question that dogged them: *Who did they play?*

Joe Paterno had inherited the head coaching job from his predecessor, Rip Engle, in 1966, and after tying Florida State in the '67 Gator Bowl, the Nittany Lions went through two straight seasons without a loss or a national championship to show for it. In 1968, they finished second behind Ohio State; in 1969, they were again mangling inferior regional competition when the Texas-Arkansas contest suddenly emerged as the third "Game of the Century" over the course of the past four seasons (one Midwest, one West, one South, zero East).

You could make a case, as many have, that this wound was also partially self-inflicted, but it's not entirely fair to do so. It's true that Penn State could have opted to play in the Cotton Bowl against the winner of Texas-Arkansas rather than in the Orange Bowl against Missouri—except this, too, was influenced by politics, as well as political timing. The Penn State players liked it in Miami, had enjoyed Miami the year before, and frankly, their black players weren't so sure about Dallas, a city where the ripples of the Kennedy assassination still lingered in many of their minds. "And . . . at the time when we were voting where we wanted to go, we were ranked third behind Ohio State[6] and Texas," Penn State quarterback Chuck Burkhart said. The Nittany Lions had already finished second in the polls the year before: At that point, they figured the best they could do was play for No. 2 again, regardless of what bowl game they chose.

Nixon and his attempts to issue a patronizing second-place plaque infuriated Joe Paterno—it still angered him years later, when queried about it following Nixon's death in 1994—but the funny thing about it is that it became perhaps the biggest turning point of Paterno's career. In the wake of the diss, Paterno spread the gospel of his "Grand Experiment," marrying academics and athletics at Penn State. By engaging toe-to-toe with a president of the United States—one he largely agreed with politically—he took on a stature as something more than a football coach, as a man with cultural cachet, a man whose opinions could be taken seriously by the university community at large. While seeking to alter his own iconography, the president had boosted Paterno's iconography (in the 1980s, Paterno, while still irritated about Nixon's slight, would tell Julie Nixon Eisenhower that he thought her father would be remembered as a great president).

"I think that differentiated Paterno from, if not all, then just about all of the coaches in the country," Edward Junker, a former

---

6. The Buckeyes, who had been dominant all season long, would lose to Michigan 24–12 in their season finale. Nixon reportedly cut a budget meeting short so he could watch his old friend Woody Hayes's team, then later had a television set up in a dental office so he could watch the finish while keeping his appointment.

chair of the Penn State board of trustees, told Sarantakes for an article published in *Pennsylvania History* magazine. "It's trite to say it, but it definitely made him a living legend as far as Penn State is concerned."

Four years after it unfolded, addressing a commencement crowd at Penn State in a soaring speech that only further elevated his place on campus, Paterno made a joke about Nixon knowing so little about Watergate in 1973 and so much about college football in 1969. It would take nearly four decades, but eventually the politics that shaped the '69 season would catch up with him, too.

V.

When it came down to it, Richard Nixon chose a hell of a college football game to attend, a game that came down to the wire—a game that may have, in fact, included the two best teams in the country that season—but what intrigues most about it all these years later is that both teams went for broke. It's almost as if they seemed determined not to get caught in the same trap that had ensnared Michigan State and Notre Dame in 1966. Here were two conservative coaches who seemed almost determined to defy their stereotypes, as if the restless mood of the nation had somehow seeped into their thinking: Trailing 14–6 after his team scored a touchdown in the third quarter, Darrell Royal chose to go for two right then and there. "If you wait until the last touchdown, it's all or nothing," Royal said, and quarterback James Street[7] ran a counter option for the conversion.

And then, facing third-and-goal in Texas territory, Arkansas chose to run a sprintout pass rather than centering the ball and kicking a field goal to go up 17–8. Some of the Arkansas players presumed that this was coach Frank Broyles making up for a previous error in judgment; a couple of years earlier, in a scoreless tie against Baylor, he'd chosen to pooch punt with time running out from the Baylor twenty-nine-yard line, and the snap had gone over the punter's head, and the Razorbacks lost 7–0, earning him the not-very-catchy nickname "Pooch Kick Frank." By 1968, Broyles had hired a progressive offensive coordinator, Don Breaux, in an attempt to implement a pro-style passing offense. Broyles did not overrule Breaux's pass call on third down, and quarterback Bill Montgomery threw an interception in the end zone, and the Longhorns got the ball back with 10:34 to play.

And finally here was Royal, facing a fourth-and-three on his own forty-three-yard line, calling a deep pass to a tight end named Randy Peschel. If it hadn't worked? "Oh man," Royal said. "I'd have been the biggest idiot of all time."

But it worked, and it picked up forty-three yards, and Texas scored the winning touchdown a few plays later, and then the president himself came into their locker room, wearing makeup for television cameras and clapping the winning coach on the back. Texas, he declared, was the undisputed No. 1 in the land,

---

7. Not to be confused with Jason Street from the *Friday Night Lights* television show, though I assume the fictional name might have been inspired by the historical name.

and then he mentioned the secondary plaque he'd bequeath to Penn State, the idea he'd formulated as Ron Ziegler scurried back and forth from the press room to the Oval Office.

"Is that fair enough?" Nixon said.

And how else could Darrell Royal, the beneficiary of the president's political largesse, reply, except to say, "Fair enough"?

VI.

That there was nothing fair about it was simply the accepted wisdom of college football in 1969, just as it had been in the decades preceding, just as it would be for decades to come. And anyway, college football was not any fairer than life itself at that moment: Five days before the game, a draft lottery was held, the first since World War II, which kind of made this whole thing feel a little less consequential.

Nixon spent the few days after the game trying to walk back his comments, to play both sides with all the interpersonal skillfulness you'd come to expect from Richard Nixon. At a press conference the Monday after the game, asked about how he might reach out to the youth of America, he made an awkward joke about *not* speaking to them by picking the No. 1 football team. Then he walked off the podium, which, I suppose, is the closest we get to Nixon dropping the mic.

The next night, addressing the National Football Foundation and Hall of Fame banquet, Nixon said Penn State should be considered for No. 1, and then, in his closing remarks, he said, "I think Texas deserved to be No. 1." Ziegler sent out letters that denied the president had declared any team the national champion, which feels like the worst kind of semantics considering that the plaque Nixon gave away explicitly declared Texas the nation's No. 1 team; still, after the Longhorns beat Notre Dame in the Cotton Bowl, thereby (at least sort of) validating Nixon's choice in both the Associated Press and United Press International polls, there wasn't much more for anyone to say. Texas had won The Argument, and everyone had settled into their respective positions, and nothing could ever be done to resolve it.

So here was yet another unsatisfactory denouement, marred by pandering and infighting and egotism. It wasn't fair at all, but such was the politics of the presidency and the politics of college football, as we had always known them to be.

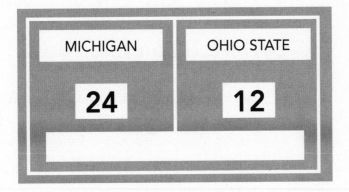

MICHIGAN	OHIO STATE
24	12

November 22, 1969

The Leaders and the Best

Discussion Topics: The Social Mechanisms of Park Forest Elementary School (Circa 1982) • Fielding Yost • Boss Weeks • Bo Schembechler • The Big Ten • Demographics • *The Big Chill* • Appalachian State • Rich Rodriguez • Headstrong Idealism

I.

"But do let me reiterate . . . the spirit of Michigan. It is based upon a deathless loyalty to Michigan and all her ways; an enthusiasm that makes it second nature for Michigan Men to spread the gospel of their university to the world's distant outposts; a conviction that nowhere is there a better university, in any way, than this Michigan of ours."

—Fielding Yost, Michigan football coach, 1941

"A Michigan Man will coach Michigan."

—Bo Schembechler, Michigan football coach, 1989

Q: "Do you have to be a Michigan Man to coach at Michigan?"
A: "Gosh, I hope not. They hired me!"

—Rich Rodriguez, Michigan football coach, 2007

II.

The first Michigan Man I knew was not yet a man at all, but I believe he was born with the necessary convictions. The first Michigan Man I knew had a surname that began with an identical syllable to mine, and so as captive prisoners of the alphabet, we were often sentenced to sit next to each other: In Hebrew School, in Mrs. Oyler's sixth-grade English class, in the dreary haze of an early-morning homeroom. On occasion, at the tail end of carpools, on empty playgrounds—in moments when we were alone and out of earshot—this M.M. was actually something resembling a friend. The rest of the time, when we were in public view, he was a towering asshole.

I don't mean that he was a bully. He was too smart for that, and he was too blandly handsome, and he was too self-aware, and he would never have resorted to something as base as physicality in order to establish his superiority over people like me. No, this M.M. was a straight-up snob, smarmy and cutting, and for mostly aesthetic reasons having to do with my hair and my glasses and my clothes, I didn't measure up to his standards.

One day at recess, I had a long discussion with M.M., and he provided a clinical breakdown of the reasons why I didn't measure up, and he explained what I could do to improve myself, and he told me why, until I did so, he felt the need to reinforce his superiority in social settings. M.M. told me all of this, laying out his case with the sociopathic calm of a character in a Bret Easton Ellis novel, as if his dickishness was a mere reflection of social mechanisms, a necessary survival instinct (which, at that age, maybe it was), and we shook hands and parted with the recognition that our relationship dynamic would never change. It was the weirdest and most revealing conversation of my childhood: He was one kind of person, he was saying, and I was another kind of person, and just because we were mandated to occupy adjacent desks didn't mean we belonged on the same plane.

We lived in Pennsylvania, but his parents were from Michigan. His father had a full head of hair and drove a sports car and looked a little like Tom Berenger's character in *The Big Chill*. (I had a low-level crush on M.M.'s sister, despite it all.) M.M. sometimes wore a Michigan sweatshirt to school, the navy one with the yellow block letters like the shirt Kevin Kline wears with his skimpy jogging shorts in *The Big Chill*. I still see that design sometimes, on T-shirts and hoodies and pullovers, and every time it transports me back to those years at Park Forest Elementary School, to a time when I first learned what it was to feel like something less than a complete human being.

All of this might well be considered a disclaimer: I am not saying M.M. is representative of all Michigan Men, and I am not saying my recollection of M.M.'s grade-school lecture is any more accurate or objective than, say, Bo Schembechler's recollections of Michigan being passed over in favor of Ohio State for the 1974

Rose Bowl bid.[1] All I'm attempting to do is confess my biases up front, and to tell you why I was hesitant to write about Michigan at all. But this is a book about college football, and so I feel like I *have* to write about Michigan. You can't ignore a Michigan Man, as much as you would like to sometimes.

III.

This notion of the Michigan Man—the idea that there's some inherent quality to those who attend and/or become associated with this particular university that cannot be replicated any- where else in the known higher-education universe, and that this concept manifests itself in the football team, with those skunk-art helmets[2] and that blue-and-yellow cut-rate superhero color scheme—began with Fielding Yost, the son of a confeder- ate soldier from West Virginia, and a natural-born bigot. It's true: The first Michigan Man harbored an open animosity for blacks and Catholics, so much so that he refused to continue to play Notre Dame after the Irish beat Michigan in 1909, so much so that he didn't have a black player of significance in his starting eleven until the 1930s (and even then, he succumbed to southern pressure and refused to play him during a game at Georgia Tech).

---

1. The vote for that berth was held by a committee of conference athletic directors after Ohio State and Michigan tied 10–10; even though Michigan dominated the game, Ohio State won the Rose Bowl bid. Schembechler, up to the day he died, called it the most bitter moment of his coaching career.

2. "Ugliest helmets in the world," Jeff Goldblum says in *The Big Chill,* and who am I to disagree?

And maybe it's unfair to start here. Maybe I should tell you that Fielding Yost's racism is not representative of the political views of the Michigan Man at large, considering that Ann Arbor is one of the most progressive communities in the Big Ten, and considering that hundreds of "student radicals" protested Yost's refusal to play Willis Ward against Georgia Tech in 1934, and considering that thousands more (including the first vestiges of the radical Weather Underground) protested the Vietnam War in Ann Arbor a few decades later. It might not even be a fair representation of Yost, given all that he did for the university over four decades, given that he apparently had a change of heart in his later years. But what he left behind was a residue of institutional arrogance that has persisted for more than a century. And I'm not saying this merely out of some deep-seated sense of childhood resentment; I'm saying this because it is how the prototypical Michigan Man views *himself*. Confidence, writes author John U. Bacon (himself a Michigan Man), is "the most important element of Michigan's identity."

Yost became the head coach at Michigan in 1901; from that season through 1905, his teams won 55 games, lost 1, and tied 1. It wasn't just that Yost's teams were nearly unbeatable: It's that they were unbeatable and stylish at the same time, putting up more than 2,800 points over that period (to their opposition's 42). Under Yost (whose nickname was Hurry Up), they ran a fast-paced offense; their quarterback during that early-twentieth-century run, Boss Weeks, would call the next play while his linemen were still pulling themselves off the ground from the play before. They would snap the ball fast, and run plays fast, and move down the field with alacrity. When opponents caught on to their rhythm, Michigan would vary the snap count, drawing an offsides penalty. It was, said one of Yost's backs, Willie "Judge" Heston, "an entirely new brand of football, not known to the Big Ten nor to the Middle West."

Yost was a teetotaler and possessed "a dull sense of humor," according to Heston. If he saw one of his players on campus, he would stop him and instruct him on blocking or tackling. Sometimes, during pregame pep talks, he would say of his opponent, "Who are they to beat a Michigan team? They're only human."

Most college football fans (myself included) are myopic and partisan; it comes with the territory. But Michigan Men don't just yearn for victory: Michigan Men believe they are *already* victorious, merely by virtue of their association with the university. The typical college football fight song, written at the turn of the twentieth century by some exuberant John Philip Sousa acolyte, is full of anachronous pleas for victory: Hold That Line, Roll Up the Score, Cheer! Cheer, Stand Up, Sing, Drink Until You Vomit.[3] But Michigan's fight song, "The Victors," perhaps the most famous fight song of them all, is also the most presumptuous. In Michigan's fight song, there are no exhortations, no prayers. In Michigan's fight song, the game has already been won.

IV.

In high school in the late 1980s, I took my first journalism class, and the highlight of the semester was the opportunity to attend

---

3. This last one is implied.

the press conference at which Penn State announced it was join-ing the Big Ten Conference. The moment itself was pretty bor-ing and platitudinous, but, even so, this was colossal news in my hometown: For decades, Penn State had played football as an eastern independent, which had contributed to the perception, in the late 1960s and early 1970s, that the Nittany Lions were an inferior program unworthy of a national championship. The thought was that membership in the Big Ten would alter this for good; the thought was that Penn State, by tethering itself to the most venerable assemblage of (largely) public universities in the country, would be able to achieve a heightened level of success.

Back then, the Big Ten still felt like something set apart from the college athletics bourgeoisie. Formed in 1895 by a consor-tium of university presidents concerned about the proliferation of "tramp athletes" who transferred from one school to another (these presidents were also interested in making money by foster-ing interstate rivalries), the Big Ten had long been the largest and haughtiest conference in college football, adhering (supposedly) to a higher academic standard, declining to offer athletic scholar-ships until their competitive hand was forced by the Southeastern Conference. In the 1930s, Minnesota was the dominant program in the land, but in the years before Penn State joined, the Big Ten had come down, in most years, to Ohio State and Michigan: the era of the Big Two and the Little Eight. The era of Woody Hayes and his onetime Miami (Ohio) player and coaching disciple, Bo Schembechler.

Woody and Bo engaged in a ten-year war of attrition (from 1969 to 1978) that resulted in only a single undisputed national championship,[4] but set the tone for what the midwestern brand of football should be: plodding and physical and beset with an undertone of rage. Woody and Bo despised each other only because they felt like they had to, given the nature of the rivalry; their outward animosity masked a deep fealty, because both men were strikingly similar, analogues of each other, Bo essentially the younger and slightly less reactionary version of Woody. (That's how it goes in college football: The best rivalries, between Ohio State and Michigan, or Auburn and Alabama, or Harvard and Yale, or Army and Navy, are based on an abiding hatred that has more to do with similarities than differences.)

For those ten years in the late 1960s and 1970s, Woody and Bo went back and forth, arguing over perceived slights, tearing up yard markers, throwing chairs, engaging in complex mind games. When Schembechler took over at Michigan in 1969, the first thing he did was tell his players that he would treat them all the same: like dogs. The first thing he did when he met his best player, offensive lineman Dan Dierdorf, was pinch his gut and say, "You're fat." The first slogan he came up with during his initial grueling spring practices was THOSE WHO STAY WILL BE CHAMPIONS, and this slogan stuck after the Wolverines beat Ohio State in '69 in one of the biggest upsets in the history of the series, and long after Bo gave way to a series of coaches who attempted (with varying amounts of success) to trade off Michigan's decade-long tradition of self-assuredness.

Late in his career, Schembechler served as the school's athletic director. When basketball coach Bill Frieder announced he'd taken

---

4. Ohio State's, in 1968.

a job at Arizona State, Schembechler fired him on the spot, declaring to the media that a Michigan Man would coach Michigan. He promoted assistant coach Steve Fisher (who was a graduate of Illinois State University, but whatever), and the Wolverines won the national championship, and in that moment, the concept of the Michigan Man was validated; no one personified the idea of the Michigan Man quite like Bo Schembechler. And it remained that way up to the day he died in 2006, the day before the second-ranked Wolverines played (and lost to) top-ranked Ohio State. Schembechler died believing that he had coached at the greatest football-playing university on earth, and that things would forever remain that way.

He died right before the fall.

V.

And so into the breach of the post Bo-Woody Big Ten era came Penn State, the conference's incongruous eleventh team. For nearly a decade, it seemed as if the Nittany Lions had made the right decision; in 1994, they went 12-0, and while they were shut out of the national championship, that helped trigger the BCS, which helped trigger the college football playoff. In 1997, Michigan won a share of the national championship,[5] and in 2002, Ohio State upset a dominant Miami team in the Fiesta Bowl to win an outright national championship. But the problem was that demographics were slowly eroding the Big Ten; the problem was that, even as the Big Ten began to explode with newfound

---

5. The best player on that team, Tom Brady, was the backup quarterback.

wealth from its cable television network, its competitive edge was slipping. For a time, this seemed like a temporary falloff, but as I write this, the downfall has lasted for a decade, and the only Big Ten team over that time with any consistent national relevance is Ohio State.[6] Which makes sense, when you look at this:

SUPPLY OF PER CAPITA FOOTBALL TALENT—
FBS ROSTERS 2011

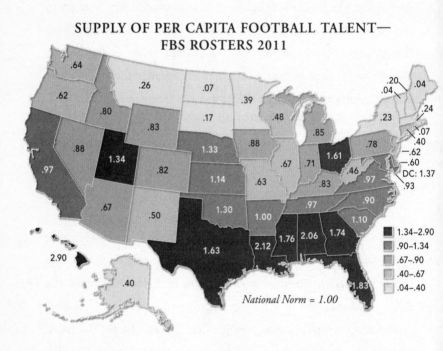

National Norm = 1.00

This chart comes from a paper presented by Theodore Goudge, an associate professor at Northwest Missouri State University, during the 2012 annual meeting of the Association of American

---

6. Which, in the process of getting hammered in two straight national championship games in the mid-2000s, essentially solidified the national perception of the conference as an entity that peaked in the pre-Watergate era.

Geographers. It pretty clearly shows what Goudge referred to as the "pigskin cult" of the South, to which the Big Ten footprint does not extend. With the glaring exception of Ohio, there is no dark gray in Big Ten country; the map only gets paler and paler the farther northeast it extends, where there are more television sets but fewer football prospects.

In case you're not convinced yet, here's another, isolating the prevalence of "blue-chip" talent:

SUPPLY OF FOOTBALL TALENT—BLUE CHIPS

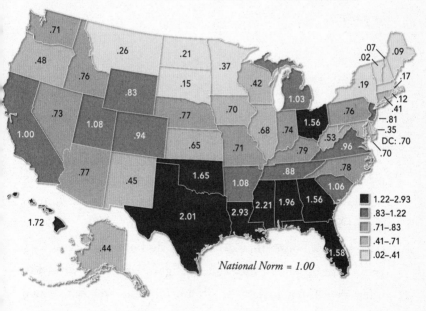

National Norm = 1.00

■	1.22–2.93
■	.83–1.22
▨	.71–.83
▧	.41–.71
□	.02–.41

The population is shifting south, where high schools practice in the spring and construct $60 million stadiums in Texas towns. Ohio, Pennsylvania, and Michigan have all shed electoral votes since 1980, while Florida and Texas have gained them. And as all of this happens, the Big Ten doesn't seem to care about much of anything except money; in 2012, they expanded and took in a pair of wayward programs, Rutgers and Maryland, largely because of their proximity to major television markets. It was a choice that made the Big Ten seem even more bloated and antiquated and Too Big to Fail than it already did in the twenty-first century. It was a choice that made me wonder if the conference of Woody and Bo—the paradigm within which the Michigan Man has long held himself superior—may only still exist because it trades so effectively off the nostalgia for a bygone era.

VI.

The Big Chill is a narcissistic and solipsistic and eminently watchable 1983 film about a group of baby boomers who met in college at the University of Michigan and are confronting their lost sense of idealism. They come together for the funeral of a friend who looks a lot like Kevin Costner,[7] they spend a weekend at a house, they drink, they do boutique drugs, they try on running shoes, they run red lights, they sleep with each other, they listen to Jeff Goldblum bloviate, and they watch Michigan play football against Michigan State. They are infuriating people with a high level of angst and self-importance,

---

7. Costner, who played the dead friend Alex in a series of flashback scenes, was famously cut out of the final version of the movie.

but they are also rampant nostalgists nearing middle age, and because I, too, am a rampant nostalgist nearing middle age, I now watch *The Big Chill* every time it is on cable. And every time I do this, and every time I watch the scene where they are watching Bo Schembechler coach a football game, and every time one of the characters says, "Don't heckle Bo, he's got enough pressure," and every time I watch the funeral scene where someone asks, "Where did Alex's hope go?" I can't help it: I think about Appalachian State.

VII.

I don't know if it is the greatest upset in modern college football history, but it may prove to be the most telling: On September 1, 2007, with time expiring, a safety named Corey Lynch burst through the line and blocked a field goal. Lynch played for Appalachian State, a Division I-AA powerhouse situated in the Blue Ridge Mountains of North Carolina; the kicker, Jason Gingell, played for Michigan, which had just lost 34–32 to Appalachian State on its home field in its season opener.

At the time, Michigan's coach was Lloyd Carr, a bland paranoiac[8] who had succeeded Gary Moeller, the man who succeeded Schembechler and then resigned after an extended public bender at a Detroit restaurant ended with him punching a police officer in the chest. Carr won that share of a national championship in

---

8. According to John U. Bacon's *Three and Out,* Carr used to go through game programs, circle the advertisements he didn't like, and ask that they be stricken. His nickname: "Paranoid Lloyd."

1997, but was never anywhere near as charismatic or as beloved as Schembechler.

After Schembechler's death in 2006, there was a palpable void among the school's alumni base, and after the Appalachian State loss led to Carr's premature retirement, Michigan hired Rich Rodriguez, the coach at West Virginia, a man who had a progressive offensive mind and an inherent inability to deal with the politics that came along with the job. The local newspaper, the *Detroit Free Press*, ran a story accusing Rodriguez of exceeding the limits of practice time; John U. Bacon's dishy book *Three and Out* chronicles the snooty insider gossip of Rodriguez's three years as coach, and essentially concludes that Rodriguez, a West Virginia guy with no direct ties to Michigan, was seen as a poor cultural fit from the moment he took the job. It's hard to say exactly why, but this may be as good a reason as any: When a university regent complained about Rodriguez's language during a speech to fans, Rodriguez had no idea what he was talking about until a staffer told him he'd used the word *ain't*. He was unadorned and unsophisticated. He tried, but he didn't measure up. He was fired after three seasons.

Rodriguez wasn't a Michigan Man, and the strict definition of this term in a modern context was hardly relevant, just as it didn't matter that Fielding Yost and Bo Schembechler were not Michigan Men until they actually *came* to Michigan to coach and started winning football games.[9] All that mattered was that this was the one thing Michigan had that no one else did, and it was imperative that their football coach fit their perception of them-

---

9. Yost, in fact, was from West Virginia.

selves.[10] Where did their hope go? Their hope went toward finding a bona fide Michigan Man (whatever the hell it meant), and
toward reliving past glories, and toward reviving the idealism of
years gone by. Their hope lay firmly in the past.

VIII.

I have no idea what happened to the M.M. who delivered that
lecture to me in elementary school. He could be a car salesman
or a movie producer or a dentist or a wealthy philanthropist or a
serial killer. I suppose it doesn't matter. I suppose my memories
of our interactions say as much about me as they do about him. I
was an awkward child, pointed inward, which was why the maps
and legends of college football appealed to me in the first place, in
the way Dungeons and Dragons appealed to other kids: By mem-
orizing the numbers on a roster, I could make myself useful. By
immersing myself in the mythology of a sport, I could dodge the
overwhelming narrative of real life. So maybe M.M. was trying to
toughen me up. Maybe he was saying, in his own crude way, that
life is about pressure, and how we handle it; maybe he was saying
that I couldn't hide within my own world forever. Maybe he was
telling me I was still young enough to change who I was.

College football, of course, is inherently a young person's pur-

---

10. Rodriguez invented a simple play called the read option (in which the quarterback either keeps the ball or hands it to a back, depending on the actions of a
defensive end), thereby helping to birth the modern spread offense. He actually
had much in common with Yost stylistically, and very little in common with him
personality-wise. He was a progressive coach at a school that now trafficked on
conservative tradition.

suit. I mean, we're all kind of stupidly arrogant at that age; it's part of the process of discovering who we are. Isn't that the whole point of college? So I imagine that's why Fielding Yost's self-absorption rubbed off on the masses in Ann Arbor, and I imagine that's why Woody and Bo's headstrong rivalry was so appealing, even to a Michigan campus riven by the Vietnam War, and I imagine the recognition of that egotism is what *The Big Chill* is really trying to capture. And I imagine that's why Michigan still matters to college football, even in an era when Michigan seems less relevant than ever before. Because at heart, the Michigan Man is just a headstrong idealist, clinging to the certitude of his youth. And it's pretty much impossible, in this day and age, to be a fan of a sport with so many inherent flaws without being an idealist.

So I get it. I understand where the Michigan Man is coming from, all these years later. They mean well, even if they sometimes express it in the worst possible ways.

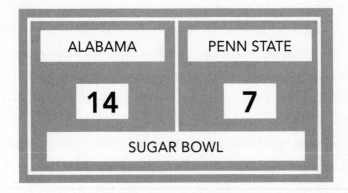

ALABAMA	PENN STATE
14	7
SUGAR BOWL	

January 1, 1979

Bear's Way

Discussion Topics: Keith Jackson • Marcel Proust • Poll Controversies • Ole Miss • USC • Michigan • The Phantom Touchdown • The Goal-Line Stand • The Length of One's Tallywhacker

I.

Everything I know about college football I view through the prism of the 1979 Sugar Bowl. It is not my earliest memory, but it might as well be: In the pale yellow American Broadcasting Corporation graphics, in the finespun play-by-play of Keith Jackson,[1] in

---

1. I don't know if it was the acoustics of the New Orleans Superdome or what, but I feel like Jackson always sounded *particularly* Jacksonesque at the Sugar Bowl—at times, it was almost overproduced, as if his voice had been filtered through Steely Dan's soundboard.

the august pro-Dixie color analysis of longtime Arkansas coach Frank Broyles, in the stark clash of the two most elegant uniforms in college football with the lime sheen of the Astroturf, in Bear Bryant's bold sartorial choice of a plaid sport jacket over a wide-collared black shirt, in the futuristic electronic time clock of the Superdome . . . hell, I guess the 1979 Sugar Bowl is my own little hyperconcussive madeleine. It triggers memories of childhood anticipation and of childhood disappointment, of every fear and obstacle and potential triumph that lay ahead; even now, when I go back to the video, the whole thing just feels so incomprehensibly huge to me, so loaded with involuntary memory—not to mention the dread of knowing how the whole thing will end—that I have trouble watching more than a few minutes at a time before I find myself shutting it off.

I was six years old when the '79 Sugar Bowl was played, and in the moment it felt like the biggest event I could ever witness. Part of it was the timing: I'd moved to a college town a few months earlier, and the university in this particular town happened to be one of the two principals involved in this game, which was being billed as an unofficial national championship contest. And because the population of my college town was perhaps one-tenth the size of Pittsburgh, this felt like our own personal Super Bowl, multiplied ten times over.

In the holiday season leading up to the '79 Sugar Bowl, it was the only thing we talked about at school. In the holiday season leading up to the '79 Sugar Bowl, I only left our basement when forced to, willing myself with a Nerf football into the bodies of Mike Guman, the Penn State tailback, and Scott Fitzkee, the Nittany Lions' wide receiver. In the holiday season leading up to the

'79 Sugar Bowl, I spent an ordinate amount of time marveling at the formidable mustache of Penn State's quarterback, Chuck Fusina, and wishing I could grow one just like it. It was the first time that I felt an overwhelming empathic attachment to a game; it was the first time the result of a sporting event felt like it might somehow serve to define *me*.

And when Penn State lost, 14–7, and when the Nittany Lions failed to push the ball across from the one-yard line in the fourth quarter, it felt like I had failed, too.

I mean, I know that sounds melodramatic (even idiotic), and I know because of the timing and the result, I've exaggerated the effect of this game in my mind. And yet I also know I am not alone in doing so. I know I am not alone in doing so because in 2002 ESPN.com ranked the 1979 Sugar Bowl as the greatest bowl game ever played, and because Keith Jackson called it the greatest game he'd ever seen in person, and because Penn State coach Joe Paterno once described the '79 Sugar Bowl as a disappointment that took him years to get over.[2] And I know I am not alone in this because I spoke to a man named James Vautravers, who was thirteen years old back then, who lived near a naval base in Omaha, Nebraska, and who was so convinced that the 1979 Sugar Bowl was the definitive national championship game of the era that he shouted down a girl from the neighborhood about it. *Of course Alabama deserved to be No. 1,* he said. *They won the national championship game on a colossal goal-line stand.*

---

2. "It got to me," he wrote in his autobiography. "It hammered at my ego. *When I stood toe to toe with Bear Bryant, he outcoached me.*"

I felt the same way, as much as it killed me to acknowledge it. And that's how I assumed it was, for more than three decades, until I started to look back at the 1978 college football season, to study the facts of that campaign instead of merely filtering them through my memory. At which point I realized, not for the first time and not for the last, that everything I thought I knew was utterly and completely colored by my own unreliable recollection of it.

II.

This is how complicated it can get when you have a sport that relies on a perpetual argument to determine its national champion: Sometimes The Argument bleeds over from one year to the next, and sometimes The Argument so obscures the truth that no one remembers it anymore. In retrospect, it seems dubious that Alabama won the Associated Press national championship for the 1978 college football season, despite what the Crimson Tide did in the '79 Sugar Bowl; in retrospect, it seems clear that Southern California, which won the coaches' (UPI) poll, had a strong case for rendering Alabama's victory moot. James Vautravers determined this years ago, when, after being challenged by that girl down the street, he went back and looked at both teams' schedules; he refined his way of thinking years later, launching a website called TipTop25, which goes back and revises the Associated Press poll rankings year by year, based on rationality and common sense rather than the whims of the moment.

And in 1978, Alabama won a national championship because the whims of the moment favored Bear Bryant.

III.

At the end of the '78 season, Joe Paterno was voted the national coach of the year, and at the banquet honoring him, he found he was seated next to Bear Bryant. At some juncture mid-meal,[3] Bryant leaned over to Paterno and said, "I hope you're going to renegotiate your contract." Paterno told him he didn't have a contract; Paterno told him he had tenure, and Bryant couldn't really grasp what that meant. Bryant said Paterno should demand more money, that he should ask for a five-year contract and a university-issued car and a country club membership, and Paterno told him he didn't play golf but Bryant kept talking, told him he should demand two hundred season tickets.

"What would I do with them?" Paterno said.

The answer, of course, was that what you did with them was irrelevant. Just the fact that you *had* them, in Bryant's mind, was what mattered. It meant you had control. It meant you had power. Bryant, Paterno explained, was "born to an old-time Southern style of politics"; he offered favors, and he used those favors to consolidate his power. People in Alabama wanted so desperately to please the Bear that his mistakes and errors in judgment were forgiven. A century after his birth, Bryant is celebrated not merely because of what he accomplished, but because of the shadow he

---

3. According to Paterno's autobiography.

cast. He may or may not be the greatest coach in college football history, but he is unquestionably the greatest political figure in college football history.

His story is rife with Lincolnesque mythology. The legend goes that Bryant wrestled a bear at age twelve; the legend goes that Bryant ran the most torturous preseason training camp in the history of football while coach at Texas A&M; the legend goes that when the Bear started recruiting black players, the segregationist movement in Alabama was essentially over. Even if these things were exaggerated, Bryant sold them as truths, like he sold himself as the truth. He was powerful enough toward the end of his career, by the time the '79 Sugar Bowl came around, that he seemed to hover above the central hypocrisies of college football. "I remember a boy sittin' right there and tellin' me, 'I just want to be like any other student,'" Bryant told author Richard Price, in a 1979 *Playboy* magazine article. "Well, shit. He can't be like any other student. The players have to take pride in the fact that football means so much to 'em."

Wrote Price, "The man could literally crush you by letting you know you were a disappointment to him."

In 1978, Alabama won a national championship because no one wanted to be a disappointment.

IV.

There are good reasons why James Vautravers feels that Alabama may have been undeserving in 1978, and it goes back, first of all, to the question of whether Alabama was deserving in 1977. That was the year the top six teams finished the season with one loss; that was the year No. 3 Alabama crushed No. 9 Ohio State in the Sugar Bowl, and No. 5 Notre Dame destroyed No. 1 Texas in the Cotton Bowl, and No. 6 Arkansas throttled No. 2 Oklahoma in the Orange Bowl, and No. 4 Michigan lost to an unranked Washington team in the Rose Bowl. That was the year a Kentucky team on probation finished 10-1, and an 11-1 Penn State team (which had lost to Kentucky) won the Fiesta Bowl over unranked Arizona State.

That was, in other words, the year the college football endgame devolved into utter chaos, and as is often the case when there is no definitive answer to The Argument, the answer became, "Notre Dame."

Did Alabama ultimately get shafted out of the 1977 national championship? Alabama partisans would say yes, because 5-6 Ole Miss handed Notre Dame its only loss of the season (20–13), and Alabama beat Ole Miss 34–13; and because Alabama, ranked third in the pre-bowl poll, won its bowl game handily, just as fifth-ranked Notre Dame did.[4] Notre Dame fans would say no, because the Irish defeated the No. 1 team in the country (Texas) in the Cotton Bowl, and defeated them 38–10, thereby deeming themselves worthy of leapfrogging; because the Irish beat USC by thirty points while Alabama beat the Trojans by one; because the Irish also defeated another top-ten team in Pittsburgh, while Alabama beat none. One pollster's retroactive rankings have the Crimson Tide fourth in '77, behind Notre Dame, Texas, and

---

4. Alabama did lose its second game of the season, to a Nebraska team that finished the season ranked twelfth in the AP poll.

Arkansas. And yet there was a sense that the Irish had crept ahead of Alabama in the final standings strictly due to politics. According to author Allen Barra's biography of Bear Bryant, several Bama players publicly commented, "No one else but Notre Dame could have gone past us."

And I have to imagine those comments lingered in the minds of Associated Press voters. I have to imagine they saw the aging visage of Bear Bryant—who collapsed in the shower from congestive heart failure before the '77 season, and checked himself into alcohol rehab after the win over Ohio State in the Sugar Bowl— and thought to themselves, *This may be the Bear's last chance. Let's not disappoint him again.*

Which, like everything else in this scenario, was an arbitrary (and ultimately untrue) assumption.

V.

Honestly, I have no real problem with split national championships. Given the impurities of the quarrels around them, I think split national championships should probably have been awarded more often than they have in the pre-playoff era. At some level, it made sense to split the national championship in '78, since Alabama defeated the consensus No. 1 team in the nation,[5] even if the Tide did not do so with the same finality that Notre Dame did the year before.

---

5. There is an entire YouTube video, a series of clips surveying the local freakout over the Tide finishing second in the coaches' poll in 1978, and the subsequent relief of the Tide winning the AP poll the next day, which kind of tells you everything you need to know about college football in Alabama.

But it also made no sense at all. And this is because of what took place on September 23, 1978, in Birmingham, Alabama: USC 24, Alabama 14.

So, just to recap: The teams that split the national championship actually played each other, during the regular season. And one team won definitively, and one team lost definitively.[6]

"To me, to break through that head-to-head loss," Vautravers said, "you'd have to have a performance advantage (over the course of the season). And Alabama didn't."

And this didn't matter at all in the end.

VI.

And here is where we get into shades of gray, and here is where we fall headlong into conspiracy theories and primordial Tuck Rule discussions, and here is where it starts to feel like the whole system is rigged, even if it's kind of hard for an impartial judge to tell who the system might actually be rigged in favor of. Here is where we start to argue about luck, which is sort of an impossible thing to argue about, unless you believe luck is not *actually* luck but is evidence of some grand oligarchical design.

Here, then, is a prime example of college football's ultimate irresolvability.

Three games, in particular, cloud the case for Southern

---

6. Oklahoma also went 11-1, with its only loss coming to a very good Nebraska team; their schedule, while difficult, was not quite as treacherous as USC's, which Vautravers calls "the toughest ever played by a team that finished #1 in one of the major polls (.663)."

Cal, in the skeptics' minds. The first, and most obvious, is USC's 20–7 loss to an unranked Arizona State team, the Trojans' only blemish of the season. That *is* damning, even if the Sun Devils, who finished 9-3, were not exactly the bottom dweller that you might assume. But beyond that, it's all based on hypotheticals, on that which perhaps *should* have happened but did not happen.

First, November 25, 1978: Notre Dame at USC. The Irish are trailing 24–6 heading into the fourth quarter, but the Irish have Joe Montana, and they take a 25–24 lead on a short Montana TD pass with forty-six seconds to play. The Trojans get the ball back on their own thirty, and quarterback Paul McDonald drops back to pass, and then . . . here's a quote from the wire service report:

> McDonald, trying to avoid a Notre Dame rush, seemed to fumble the football. But the officials ruled he had begun forward motion of his arm and called the play an incomplete pass.

So USC keeps the ball, and McDonald completes a thirty-five-yard pass on the next play, and the Trojans kick a field goal to win the game.

And it doesn't end there. Because on New Year's Day, USC plays Michigan in the Rose Bowl, and Charles White dives for the end zone from the three-yard line, and the ball comes loose, and appears to come loose well before White actually reaches the end zone. Michigan fans refer to it as the "Phantom Touchdown"; their indignation, in this case, appears to be well-placed, as the officials were quite clearly confused. And this is where the con-spiracy theorists find their grist: because even though the official who initially ruled in favor of USC was actually a Big Ten official from Chicago (name of Gil Marchman), the referee who made the final determination was a Californian (and Pac-8 official) named Paul Kamanski. And Kamanski, reportedly succumbing to Marchman's adamance about White's forward progress, ruled the play a touchdown.

And USC won, 17–10.

And Paul Kamanski, as it turned out, was the same referee who presided over the USC–Notre Dame game.[7]

VII.

We could play these little mind games forever, if we wanted; for instance, there is a YouTube video of a blatant hold that was not called on one of Alabama's touchdowns in the '79 Sugar Bowl. But there are some things I am willing to admit here, even as a Penn State partisan, and one is that, of the three teams in contention for the national championship that day, Penn State had played the weakest schedule[8]; the other is that

---

7. Kamanski later became a pioneer of instant replay in the USFL and the NFL, which I'm assuming the black-helicopter crowds in Ann Arbor and Tuscaloosa and South Bend would ascribe to a guilty conscience.

8. USC played the toughest schedule in the nation that year, according to poll-ster Richard Billingsley. The Trojans faced seven teams that finished in the AP or coaches' top twenty, while Alabama faced four (Penn State played three); and USC played six road games compared to Alabama's three. In terms of strength of schedule, there's no real comparison.

the Nittany Lions blew a clear opportunity to erase any doubt over the '78 season by failing to gain a single yard when they absolutely had to.

It really is a remarkable goal-line stand, when you look back at it. On second-and-goal, Fusina throws an out to Fitzkee, who appears to have a clear path to six points until cornerback Don McNeal streaks in from the deep blue of the Superdome end zone and railroads him out of bounds. On third down, Matt Suhey leaps over the top and goes nowhere. And then it's fourth down, and as Paterno wrote in his autobiography, "I called a time-out and told my coaches I wanted [Fusina] to fake a run and throw a little pop pass to the tight end."

But his coaches argued against him. His coaches argued for conservatism. His coaches said, *If we can't gain a yard, we don't deserve the national championship,* and Paterno acquiesced. He handed the ball to Mike Guman, and Guman leapt above the pile, high into the air, and was stood up by a linebacker named Barry Krauss, who pinched a nerve in his neck and broke a chip off his helmet and had no idea what happened on the play until his teammates told him. Years later, they still sell posters of Barry Krauss standing up Mike Guman on the goal line, and ostensibly winning Alabama the national championship by a stretch of turf that Bryant later estimated, to a reporter, was "about the length of your tallywhacker."

I look back at that goal-line stand, and I like to think I learned all sorts of valuable lessons: that life cannot be lived conservatively, that failure must be accepted, that disappointment is inevitable. I look back at that goal-line stand and I wonder, sometimes, if it shaped my worldview more than I'd like to admit.

And so that game will always *feel* like a behemoth to me, obscuring everything in its wake. But then, this is what the Bear did better than any other football coach who ever lived; he made everything around him appear bigger than it actually was. He did this, in part, by playing the game outside of the game, by courting favors and prostrating himself when necessary and elevating himself when necessary. In the fall of '78, at the behest of the Sugar Bowl committee, Bryant phoned Joe Paterno, angling for a place in a matchup that would determine the national championship. "You know, Joe," he said,[9] "we aren't worth a lot, really, and somebody is going to beat us. I'd like for it to be a good team like yours to do that when it happens."

Joe Paterno agreed. The Bear exerted control over the situation. And Alabama won the 1978 national championship because the whims of the moment favored Bear Bryant.

VIII.

I have a photo in my home office, a black-and-white shot of the Bear standing against a goalpost at Penn State's Beaver Stadium during pregame warm-ups, legs crossed, game plan rolled up in his hands, his jacket plaid, his turtleneck white, his hat houndstooth and pulled low over his eyes. There is nothing happening

---

9. According to Allen Barra's biography of Bryant.

in the photo; it is just a picture of an old man leaning against a slab of metal, and I could stare at it for hours.

This is what the Bear does. He *looms.* He is there, looming over us all, even now, decades after his death, passing judgment on me as I prepare to type the following sentence.[10] And yet I'm going to type it anyway: I'm no longer convinced that Alabama deserved to win the 1978 national championship. All I can say for certain is that Penn State lost it. Even if the Nittany Lions score right there, with six minutes to play, and they choose to tie the game at 14, and they finish 11-0-1, it would have been nearly impossible to make the case against them; if Penn State gains one yard, there is no real debate at all about the '78 national champion.

(Sometimes, there is no claim in The Argument at all. Sometimes, you just lose.[11])

The goal-line stand, then, is Alabama's best case for a share of the title: When forced to face up directly against their own obsolescence, the Crimson Tide did not fold. That's all The Argument of '78 is about. It is rooted in the persistence of memory; it is rooted in the legacy of the Bear himself. I refer you to an on-air "commentary" (available on YouTube) from an Alabama television anchor after the release of the UPI poll: It begins with a callback to what happened the year before, in 1977, with Notre Dame, and to the idea that defeating a No. 1

---

10. "We already got a perfectly good system in college football," Bryant once said. "It's called a regular season. Anything that ain't settled by the end of it plus one bowl game should stay unsettled."

11. Or sometimes you just win: In 1979, Alabama went 12-0, while USC went 11-0-1, and the Tide earned a pretty clear consensus national championship.

team trumps even the idea of losing to the team that has equal claim to No. 1; it clings to the idea that "hype" (in the form of media credential requests, I guess) should play a central role, that a national championship game *becomes* a national championship game when it is made to feel like something larger than life. Which, in the end, is exactly how I remember it.

MIAMI	NEBRASKA
31	30
ORANGE BOWL	

January 2, 1984

The Resolution Will Be Televised

Discussion Topics: Tom Osborne • Enemas • Two-Point Conversions • Turner Gill • Bowl Executives • The History of Tiebreakers • Nebraska 62, Florida 24 • Zero-Sum Football

I.

In 1985, in the aftermath of the boldest single decision any college football coach has ever made, the man who made that decision published an autobiography titled *More Than Winning*. It is a volume that somehow manages to be both brief and tedious, short on telling detail about the author's career as the head coach of a major college football team and long on religious platitudes and recountings of post-heart-surgery hospital enemas.[1] The book is dedicated in part to the Creator and thanks the Lord in the acknowledgments, in case He didn't get the message the first time. In the opening paragraph of the foreword, the author admits that the publishing company contacted him, and that he "had many reservations" about writing a book at all.

This is no one's fault, really. Tom Osborne, the longtime coach of the Nebraska Cornhuskers, is a proudly undynamic guy whose long-term success has come to embody the spirit of one of the most proudly undynamic states in the union (which Osborne also served as a congressman).[2] The penultimate chapter in the book, "A Difficult Road to Walk," is an in-depth exploration of Osborne's Christianity—he notes that he never infringes on Sundays during the season, so his players can attend services, "Protestant, Catholic *or Jewish*"[3]—and this chapter is far longer than his description of the thrilling Orange Bowl game played the year before, which is pretty much the only reason an autobiography of a midcareer college football coach from a sparsely populated state who had not yet won a national championship would be desired by a major publisher in the first place.

---

1. The book jacket promises that what lies inside is "more than an autobiography, more than sports, more than a philosophy. It is honesty. It is integrity. It is inspiring." All of which sounds more *Yeezus* than Jesus.

2. I recently had a dinner-party conversation about the least interesting state in the union; Nebraska was a finalist, but was eliminated from contention because A) it splits its electoral votes for the presidency, and B) the Cornhuskers. "The most important thing in this state is Nebraska football," the university's sports information director once said. "The second most important thing in this state is Nebraska spring football."

3. The italics are mine. The lack of Shabbat knowledge is Osborne's.

As far as I can tell, Osborne never gets to the point of explaining the rationale behind his most significant coaching decision in *More Than Winning*.[4] But I like to think he is purposefully vague about it because he prefers to speak in parables, which is what you'd expect from a man who nearly went into the seminary after college. I'd like to presume that the rest of the book, with its folksy yarns about Osborne's upbringing in small-town Nebraska—in particular, the anecdote about Osborne's grandfather, who once lost a political election because he literally refused to campaign—is meant to tell us everything we need to know about Tom Osborne's state of mind on the second evening of January in 1984, when he went for broke and failed in spectacular and very public fashion.

"I was disappointed," Osborne writes about this failure, "and yet it was certainly not a shattering experience."

If almost any other football coach said this in an autobiography, I would assume he never actually bothered to read his own (obviously ghostwritten) book. But this is what set Tom Osborne apart during all those years as head coach at Nebraska: He really did seem to exist on his own spiritual plane, set apart from the egotism that drives most of the men in his profession. He was such an overpowering believer in the Christian arc of sin and redemption that he occasionally gave too much leeway to those who didn't

---

4. It's kind of astounding to realize that a man as platitudinous as Osborne has written *three* autobiographies, but for an explanation, I refer you back to the quote in footnote number 2.

deserve it.[5] Even after his periodic character misjudgments, even after an unremarkable political career, Osborne remains the paragon of Nebraskan virtue—his approval rating in the state *after* he lost a gubernatorial election, according to a 2011 Public Policy Polling survey, was 86 percent, making him "the most popular person PPP has ever polled on anywhere."

Some of this, of course, is due to the fact that Tom Osborne was a remarkably successful football coach, especially later in his career. But really, only a man so confident in the karmic arc of the universe could have made the decision that Osborne did in 1984, and only a man who was willing to *subvert* politics could have survived the repercussions of that decision with the dignity that Tom Osborne did (which is why his move into real-life politics always seemed more like a default move than one based on passion). He had a national championship in hand, the easy way, if he wanted it. But Osborne refused to reduce the national championship to a campaign. He worked around The Argument that had defined the sport since its earliest days. And in so doing, he struck another blow in the long fight to cleave The Argument to pieces.

---

5. Osborne allowed running back Lawrence Phillips back on the team in 1995 after he was arrested for assaulting his ex-girlfriend. Osborne insisted that the "structure" of organized football was Phillips's best hope for rehabilitation; Phillips is currently serving a thirty-year prison sentence. Several other players on Osborne's mid-1990s national championship teams also had criminal records, including nose tackle Christian Peter, who was accused of multiple sexual assaults and was arrested eight times, including once for threatening to kill a parking attendant.

II.

There are some inherently notable obstacles that hindered then-undefeated Nebraska in the final moments of the 1984 Orange Bowl, trailing one-loss Miami 31–24, with a minute and forty-seven seconds to play. The first is that Nebraska is attempting to overcome this deficit against the Hurricanes' home crowd in Miami. A coach with a more combative nature than Osborne might have argued that the nation's No. 1 team—a squad that had averaged fifty-two points per game and was already being acknowledged as perhaps the greatest unit of all time—probably didn't deserve to play a road game for the national championship. The second obstacle is that the Cornhuskers were without Mike Rozier, who, in retrospect, may be the best running back in college football history; he was on the bench, his ankle sprained,[6] while his team drove downfield for the potential game-tying/game-winning score.

The third notable obstacle on this drive is Irving Fryar. Irving Fryar, of course, played for Nebraska. Irving Fryar may be the finest wide receiver in Cornhuskers history. But something weird happens here, and I'm not even sure how to talk about it without casting aspersions on Fryar himself—I have no proof of any foul play, and I'm not sure anyone else does, either—but I have never seen a receiver of Fryar's prodigious ability drop a pass in the way he does in the midst of this drive. There he is, streaking across the middle of the field, wide open in the end

---

6. Rozier later admitted to "having a few beers" with executives from the USFL's Pittsburgh Maulers during game week. He said these conversations didn't affect his play; he also said, "I feel bad about losing. But you can't win them all."

zone, and Nebraska's quarterback, Turner Gill, hits him directly in the hands, and Fryar seems to bat the ball away as if he's fighting off a rabid squirrel. (Equally strange: Fryar goes to the ground in the back of the end zone, hands to his helmet, in what I'll just assume is a moment of genuine self-pitying introspection, and a gang of Orange Bowl executives—they're the guys in the stupidly hued sport coats—leap up and down and celebrate right next to him. You want a five-second exposé on the inherent corruption of college football's postseason system, you could seize on that moment right there.)

The fourth notable obstacle on this drive: Facing a fourth-and-eight, the game on the line, Osborne runs the ball. Technically, it was a play called 41 sprint pass, a run-throw quarterback option, but there was really only one option for Gill to throw to, and that was Fryar running a slant. And given what had just happened a moment before, the only viable option for Gill was to keep the damn thing himself, which he did, pitching at the last moment to a second string I-back named Jeff Smith, who careened around the edge of the line and down the sideline and into the end zone on the kind of crazy play that no coach would have the cojones to execute in today's modern game.

The fifth notable obstacle on this drive, of course, is Osborne himself. When his team scores those six points, he does not hesitate. It's clear he had made up his mind long ago: He would go for two points here.[7] He would not settle, as Ara Parseghian had done while at Notre Dame years before; he would not put this in

---

7. "I don't think any of our players would be satisfied backing into it with a PAT," Osborne said earlier in the week.

the hands of the poll voters, even though those poll voters would have almost certainly rewarded him with a title merely for mustering a tie game in a hostile stadium with a team that had scored more points than any squad since 1944.

Osborne didn't seem to factor any of this into his thinking. He went for the two. He went for the outright victory, wrote one newspaper columnist, "in a rare display of courage, arrogance and selfishness." He lined up three receivers to the right, and Gill threw in the flat to Smith, and the pass was tipped away, and Osborne's gambit failed, and Miami won the national championship.

And no coach has ever succeeded, or probably ever will, by failing to the extent that Osborne did, in that moment.

Years later, when Armen Keteyian wrote a muckraking book that examined Rozier's possible cocaine use and questioned whether Fryar might have been involved in throwing the Orange Bowl, Osborne said, "[F]or years Nebraskans have felt that I was predictable, unimaginative, too nice a guy, unemotional and all these types of things. And here's a guy [Keteyian] who comes from New York City, big-time writer, analyst of human behavior, and he says I'm mysterious and a man of conflicting emotions. I hope Nebraskans will sit up and take notice of that."

I have no idea if he was joking. But I imagine that at least within the state of Nebraska, Tom Osborne became far more interesting than he actually was, merely because of the choice he made in Miami that night.

III.

The NFL introduced overtime for divisional tiebreaking games in 1940, and overtime for championship games in 1946, and sudden-death overtime for regular-season games in 1974. In Kansas, overtime rules for high school football were adopted in 1971. And through it all, thanks largely to the besotted fools in sport coats who danced on Irving Fryar's skull in that end zone in 1984, college football changed nothing.

More than twenty times between 1869 and 1990, the "consensus" national champion played to at least one tie; Princeton is recognized by several sources as the No. 1 team in 1881, despite playing to two ties. In 1946 and 1966, most notably, the national championship was awarded to Notre Dame after a tie game. As is so often the case in college football, the status quo remained long past its due date, largely because it 1) reinforced the stature of the bowl system, and 2) reduced pressure on the coaches. It was one less decision to make. Sometimes, a tie felt like a victory; the lingering presence of the two-point conversion made it seem as if there *was* a tiebreaking method,[8] even though there were situations when the two-point conversion didn't come into play at all.

And so college football did not approve overtime until 1996, adopting the Kansas high school rules. Even then, the tie was only truly abandoned for reasons of commerce: The tie made it more difficult for a team to garner the six wins necessary to qualify for a bowl game. And now that college football had something called a

---

8. "I thought we had the two-point play for that reason," said Joe Paterno, when overtime rules were approved in 1996.

bowl alliance, which would potentially match the top two teams, a tie game no longer seemed like a rational and/or desirable result.

It feels kind of quaint now, to think that college football held out for so long. Part of what explains the endurance of The Argument is the fact that the college game has tried so hard to maintain its unique identity, even if it comes at the expense of the people who actually watch it. There is only one good point to be made in favor of the tie game, and this is that coaches will "play for overtime" late in games, that they will tend toward conservatism, that they will put off making any sort of controversial decision until they absolutely have to. And it's true: This does happen now. Coaches consistently play for overtime.

But it happened before, too, when overtime didn't even exist.

In an ideal world, every coach might have made the choice Tom Osborne did rather than playing for the tie; it took Osborne actually *doing* it to make us realize that most coaches were actually perfectly happy with the tie game if it made them look okay in the end. It took Tom Osborne to help us realize that the politics of college football were inherently absurd.

IV.

"If I was sure a tie would make me No. 1 in the polls," Ara Parseghian told the Associated Press the day after the Orange Bowl, "I would rather be ranked No. 1. Five, 10, 15 years from now, that's what people will remember—that you were the top team in the country."

And this is one thing that Ara, in playing for that tie against

Michigan State in 1966, got wrong: The majority of people found Osborne's choice inherently noble. It is one case where a loss actually proved *better* than a win. Miami would go on to win other titles, and so would Nebraska, but that loss shaped Osborne's legacy; in 1994, when the Cornhuskers went undefeated and Penn State went undefeated, Nebraska was awarded its first championship, largely because Osborne had yet to win one.[9] (He won again the next year, fielding one of those most dominant teams in college football history: The '95 Huskers put up an average of fifty-two points per game, pounded second-ranked Florida in the Fiesta Bowl, 62–24, and trailed only once all season. All of that kind of retroactively invalidated the whole lifetime-achievement-award angle in '94.)

"I was totally on board with the two-point conversion," says my friend Bob Ethington, who was born in Omaha and grew up a Nebraska fan. "It seemed the right and noble thing to do. When it failed, it was terrible, but I can't say that I really second-guessed Osborne's decision (nor have I since). Rather, I admired him for it. But as I think about it now—I would never support such a decision today. It would drive me crazy! And that realization makes me a little sad."

Osborne's choice did not alter anything overnight, because college football seems to pride itself on the glacial nature of its

---

9. You could make a case that Nebraska deserved to win the national championship in 1983, despite the loss to Miami. You could also make a case for Auburn, which went 11-1 and according to poll historian James Vautravers, played the fourth-toughest schedule in college football history. (Another pollster, Richard Billingsley, has Auburn No. 1 in his retroactive rankings; Miami is fourth, behind the Georgia Bulldogs—who lost to Auburn and tied Clemson 16–16—and the Texas Longhorns, who lost to Georgia in the Cotton Bowl. Nebraska is fifth.)

decision-making process. But it moved us steadily forward, toward the realization that the current system was inherently flawed and purposefully nebulous—that it almost seemed designed to punish those who pushed for any sort of definitive resolution. It set us on a path toward overtime and toward the BCS and eventually toward a playoff system, and it rewarded Osborne with a lifetime of solid karma from the people of his state.

But I think my friend Bob is right. I think no coach in his right mind, faced with the Osborne Conundrum, would make this choice now. To give up a near-certain national championship in the polls for a shot at . . . what? A more *definitive* national championship? It sounds like a cautionary tale from an overconfident statistician. The consequence of failure would be seismic; in certain regions of the country, it might even cost a coach his job. This is the uncomfortable truth about a sport that, like so many other things, has slowly evolved from The Argument model to the zero-sum model: There is nothing *More Than Winning*. Three decades later, Tom Osborne's decision strikes me as both inherently laudable and sadly anachronistic.

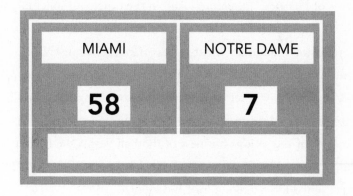

MIAMI	NOTRE DAME
58	7

November 30, 1985

In the Air Tonight

Discussion Topics: Jim Kelly • Howard Schnellenberger • Jimmy Johnson • Sonny Crockett • Reaganomics • The 1987 Fiesta Bowl • *Red Dawn* • Southern Methodist University • Wide Right I • Bobby Bowden • 2 Live Crew • Insurrection

I.

I can recall the very moment that the Miami Hurricanes became a threat to the social order of college football: It was 1981, and I was nine years old, and it was Halloween. We were hustling door-to-door in packs, dressed up as fedora-wearing archaeologists and flannel-bedecked moonshine runners and mini Brent Musburgers,[1] thrusting outstretched pillowcases at the waists of neighbors toting bowls of Hershey's miniatures. And in the process of soliciting, we would also inquire as to the score. No one needed to be told *what* score; it was a Saturday night in State College, Pennsylvania, and Penn State was ranked No. 1 in the nation, playing on the road at Miami. In any other circumstance, I would have been at home watching the game on television or listening on the radio[2]; it was a matter of the serious business of football versus the frivolity of childhood, and in that moment, I'm kind of ashamed to admit that I opted to go looking for Mr. Goodbar.

History tells me there were thirty-two thousand people in the Orange Bowl that night, amid a driving rainstorm. The home team's quarterback was Jim Kelly, a junior from a small Pennsylvania town who would go on to the Pro Football Hall of Fame; Joe Paterno, the Penn State coach, had attempted to recruit him as a linebacker, which, in retrospect, might have been a mistake. The Hurricanes had gone 42-67 throughout the 1970s, and they'd never finished better than 6-5 in the decade. Their program was moribund and underfunded, their facilities so laughably terrible that they avoided giving tours to their own recruits. And then in came a mustachioed Bear Bryant disciple named Howard Schnel-

---

1. Though that may have only been me: I dressed up in a suit as the CBS Sports announcer, using my violin case as a proxy for an actual camera, which is the most utility I ever got out of two years of attempting to decipher that goddamned instrument.

2. Until the deregulation of college football broadcasts and rise of ESPN in the mid-1980s, a lot of Penn State's road games weren't televised at all. And so we'd listen on the radio to the charmingly partisan call of the local announcers; the color commentator, for many years, was Joe Paterno's brother, George, who so mimicked the garbled Brooklynese syntax of his sibling that you couldn't tell them apart.

lenberger, who was only forty-four in 1981 but smoked a pipe and wore a jacket and tie in the July heat and looked like a veteran of the Spanish-American War.

Miami had defeated a mediocre Penn State team in 1979 on the road, but this was different. This was a Penn State team with Todd Blackledge at quarterback and Curt Warner at running back, a Penn State team with legitimate national championship aspirations. The night before the game, speaking to *Sports Illustrated*'s William Nack, Schnellenberger said, "I took this job with the idea of building a national champion." He said he hoped Miami's athletic program would someday compare with those of Southern Cal and Notre Dame and Penn State; he said if Miami could pull out a victory, the country would know the Hurricanes were for real.

And so at one of the last houses of the night, pillowcases sagging, oversized costumes slipping down to our shoes, we were told the final score: Miami 17, Penn State 14.

Things accelerated quickly after that. Two years later, led by a freshman quarterback with an African-American hairdo and a Jewish delicatessen owner's name,[3] the Hurricanes won their first national championship. Schnellenberger departed, lured by the ephemeral riches of the United States Football League for a head coaching position that dematerialized before he would coach a single game. As a replacement, the Hurricanes hired the head coach at Oklahoma State, an impeccably coiffed psychology major named Jimmy Johnson.

Johnson was slick and brilliant and merciless. He was, I sup-

---

3. Bernie Kosar was actually a white Catholic from Youngstown, Ohio.

pose, the embodiment of Miami itself, a city that was Day-Glo and troubled and noirish enough that it inspired the defining prime-time detective program of the era. In 1985, in the season finale of his second year at the helm, the Hurricanes faced a floundering Notre Dame squad, headed by lame-duck coach Gerry Faust. They kept throwing the ball, and kept scoring touchdowns, and kept laying it on. Up in the broadcast booth, former Notre Dame coach Ara Parseghian pleaded for Johnson to "show some compassion"; after Miami blocked a punt and scored a touchdown in the final minutes, play-by-play man Brent Musburger chastised Johnson for "humiliating" the Irish.

Miami won, 58–7. A defiant Johnson refused to apologize for any of it.

And after that, college football never looked quite the same again.

II.

"Confidence is necessary to play football. Different players have different ways of building confidence. Both my formal training in psychology and my decades of firsthand experience with human beings told me that if I stymied and handcuffed the players who needed to be demonstrative, I would stymie and handcuff their confidence. Because of a lot of our players' backgrounds, we had to be somewhat flamboyant. . . . I don't know that there was racism involved in the resentment, but there was some ignorance involved—people who had few dealings with other ethnic groups."

—Jimmy Johnson

"You've got to know the rules before you can break 'em. Otherwise, it's no fun."

—Sonny Crockett, *Miami Vice*

III.

On the second evening of January in 1987, Miami played Penn State in the Fiesta Bowl for the national championship. It was a game so fraught with off-field tension that it became the highest-rated college football broadcast in history. It was a big deal everywhere— President Reagan spoke to NBC at halftime, wearing a cardigan and sharing circuitous stories that harked back to the days of the Gipper—but for me, and for my hometown, this game felt like a referendum on who we actually were.

Miami's players disembarked from the team plane wearing combat fatigues, thereby sparking a widespread sartorial freak-out among the media. Penn State's Joe Paterno had been named *Sports Illustrated*'s Sportsman of the Year the week before, and the perception of him as a football coach possessed of unparalleled integrity would never be greater than at that moment. Miami's players stormed out of a friendly pregame barbecue, comparing themselves to the Japanese the night before Pearl Harbor (a peculiar metaphor, one Penn State player noted, given the way the war turned out). All of it made for a quint-essential 1980s narrative, a Schwarzenegger film in miniature: For reasons that seemed self-evident to me at the time, Penn State became the white hats and Miami became the black hats. Miami's players were faster and more athletic and more demonstrative and just better in every imaginable way, and while Penn State had its share of black players, too, the racial implications of these assigned roles seem dumbfoundingly obvious in retrospect (so much so that the same Penn State player who made the Pearl Harbor quip, punter John Bruno, also joked that the Nittany Lions let their black players eat at the training table with them once a week).

When Penn State won 14–10, intercepting Miami quarterback Vinny Testaverde five times, throttling the Hurricanes' purposefully cocky receivers to the point that they began to drop passes in anticipation of what hits might be coming, it felt like both a miracle and a validation. For years, it was my favorite football game of all time, a reinforcement of everything I loved about my hometown and my alma mater and the modest principles of Anywhere, U.S.A. And it was only twenty-five years later, when the defensive coordinator who devised Penn State's impeccable game plan turned out to be one of the most notorious pedophiles in modern history,[4] that I began to question every assumption I'd ever made about the narrative of that evening.

I don't think college football ever served as a social bellwether quite like it did in the 1980s. And I realize it's possible I just viewed it that way because of geography and circumstance. I realize it's possible that college football became a conduit for

---

4. In 2012, Jerry Sandusky was convicted on forty-five counts of child sexual abuse and sentenced to thirty to sixty years in prison.

my social development because 1) I was at a particularly impressionable age, and 2) I lived in a college town where the football team had become the focal gauge of the community's values.

This college town I grew up in was not progressive like Berkeley or Austin; it wasn't defined by highbrow intellectualism like Princeton or Palo Alto. We didn't have film festivals or alternative radio stations or communist bookstores or Indian restaurants; we had a classic rock station and a video arcade called Playland and fourteen sub shops and long lines for *Red Dawn*. This college town was nestled in the mountains of central Pennsylvania, a good three-to-four-hour drive away from at least five major American cities, with a one-terminal airport (upgraded from a double-wide trailer) and a surrounding population that was almost entirely white. The divide between town and gown was glaring and often uncomfortable; one-fourth of my high school graduating class didn't show up at school on the first day of deer-hunting season, and one-fourth was enrolled in advanced calculus courses at the university to burnish their Yale applications. The primary divide was between "jocks" and "hicks," between the upper-middle-class progeny of academics and the working-class progeny of farmers. Racism wasn't an overt issue because there weren't enough people of color around to make it an issue.

I did not come from a conservative family—my parents may have been the only people on our block who openly voted for Mondale in '84—but when it came to college football, I was a staunch reactionary. Everybody around me was, too. This was the paradigm of Penn State, and of Joe Paterno, and hence of the town itself: plain uniforms, a lack of tolerance for the demonstrative on-field behavior that had become Miami's trademark, and a professed fealty to the idea of reconciling academics and athletics that didn't seem a priority in most other places in the mid-1980s—at Miami, at Oklahoma, at Georgia, and in virtually the entire Southwest Conference, where players were paid with fat envelopes of hundred-dollar bills delivered from the offices of Texas oilmen and appeared to have virtually no educational responsibilities. They were football players who happened to attend college, and they made no apologies for it.

"I'm glad we did it," one Miami player said after the blowout of Notre Dame in 1985. "I don't feel sorry about it."

Comments like this perplexed me. I was a white kid of middle-class privilege who had spent most of his life in a small town known to outsiders as Happy Valley. I couldn't understand why everyone didn't at least attempt to exist within the rules. It wasn't that I hated Miami so much as they seemed to exist on a plane beyond my comprehension.

IV.

Two months before that '87 Fiesta Bowl game, a Dallas television station aired an interview with a former Southern Methodist University football player named David Stanley. It was thorough and damning, even though Stanley's testimony was colored by the ongoing drug issues that would eventually lead to his death. The television report centered around an envelope, and this envelope bore the official watermark of SMU, and the initials of SMU assistant athletic director Henry Lee Parker. Stanley alleged that he had been paid $400 a month to play at

SMU, and that he had been mailed an additional $350 every month to cover his car payments. The station hired a handwriting analyst, who said she was confident enough that she would testify in court that Parker had marked the envelope. And then they interviewed a shaky and confused Henry Lee Parker, who, rather than deny everything, confirmed that it *was* his handwriting on the envelope.

This was the end. This was the moment that killed the SMU program for a generation to come, the breaking open of a vast conspiracy of silence that rose all the way up to the office of the governor of the state of Texas. This was college football's Watergate; the Mustangs, who repeatedly and defiantly continued to pay their players even after being caught the first time, became the first (and still the only) NCAA football program to receive the NCAA's death penalty, a two-year hiatus without any games at all. And with this came yet another flood of angst about the disproportionate place of college sports on campus, about the rampant corruption in the Southwest Conference that SMU belonged to, about how maybe college football had become a reflection of a materialistic society and about how maybe the whole enterprise was doomed to its own personal hell. It was the same kind of hand-wringing that had taken place at the turn of the twentieth century, with one twist: This time, certain fundamental truths were acknowledged.

"I'm not afraid to say it: It's a business," Florida State athletic director Hootie Ingram told the *New York Times*.

That this qualified as a controversial quote in 1986 is one measure of just how far things have come. And for that, we have the rule breakers to thank.

V.

There's a moment that arises after the kick slips a couple of feet wide to the right, after Miami's flop-footed ibis[5] mascot charges onto the field, after the camera flashes the now-iconic image of a flummoxed Florida State coach Bobby Bowden, hands on hips, head swiveling from side to side like a man who has just watched the last crosstown bus of the evening pass him by. There's a moment that crops up at the ending of 1991's iteration of the Game of the Century, after Keith Jackson utters seven words—"It's up . . . missed it to the right!"—and after the ABC broadcast gives way to several seconds of ambient noise. It is a moment I find fascinating, and it arrives when Jackson speaks up again, after Miami's entire sideline, along with what seems like half the population of Coral Gables, fans out across the landscape of Florida State's Doak Campbell Stadium in celebration of an imminent 17–16 victory over the Seminoles. And what Jackson says is such a brilliant single-sentence summation of the Hurricanes' decade of college football dominance that I'm surprised someone didn't have it copyrighted, printed up on bumper stickers, and distributed at every Foot Locker from Hollywood to Homestead.

"Miami players are all over the field, they're going to be penalized for it," Jackson says. "But '*So what*' I'm sure is their attitude."

It was November 16, 1991, in Tallahassee, Florida, one of the

---

5. His given name is Sebastian, but just because the university insists that he is modeled after a long-legged wading bird in the family of Threskiornithidae does not mean he doesn't resemble a sleazed-out Howard the Duck after a night of Courvoisier.

last afternoons of the Miami dynasty. The season would end with Miami winning a share of the national championship, its fourth since 1983. But there were scandals in progress and scandals waiting to be unveiled, scandals involving purveyors of sexually explicit rap lyrics[6] and bounty payments and the manipulation of Pell Grant funds; by '91, the program was on the cusp of deteriorating from a revolutionary force into an anarchic state, thereby fulfilling all the racially tinged prophecies of sports columnists who viewed the Hurricanes as a metaphor for the coarsening of American culture throughout the eighties.[7] Jimmy Johnson had departed for the professional ranks, giving way to Dennis Erickson, a passive authority figure[8] who was simply not equipped to maintain control of a program that had been built on a foundational attitude of *So what?* (Erickson, too, would soon depart for the professional ranks).

By 1991, one might argue, there was no realistic way to exert control over a program that had been designed on the premise of subverting the system itself. And this was the problem with Jimmy Johnson's psychological tactics: Eventually that confidence

---

6. Luther "Luke Skywalker" Campbell, the creative force behind 2 Live Crew, a band now remembered as much for being terrible as for being controversial, was one of Miami's most prominent boosters for years.

7. Sample quote, from legendarily cranky columnist Bernie Lincicome: "I am not without some gratitude for Miami collecting dangerous young thugs and giving them a place to be angry. Better in Coral Gables than on public transportation."

8. Before a game against Florida A&M in 1992, Erickson upheld a team vote against a pregame handshake. By that point, he was so stressed out about coaching at Miami that his face broke out with fever blisters before games.

he'd bred became endemic.[9] The Hurricanes had already booted old-fashioned notions of sportsmanship in the face during the previous year's Cotton Bowl: Amid a 46–3 rout of Texas, they racked up more than two hundred yards in penalties. Nineteen ninety-one, school officials insisted, would be the year Miami "cleaned itself up," conforming to the anti-celebration rules the NCAA instituted after the Cotton Bowl.

And yet these Hurricanes were still boisterous and wild, and what had Florida State done at that point but openly co-opted Miami's institutional bluster in order to lure the same base of recruits?

This game—which would come to be known, in the annals of Florida football, as Wide Right I[10]—would clear a path to Miami's fourth national championship in nine years, and the last of that era of dominance. And the first thing you notice when you watch the highlights of Wide Right I is the ferocity; the number of hits that would be flagged today as excessive and dangerous is near astronomical. The second thing you notice is that time has not dimmed the recognition that this was incredibly advanced football.

There were, as Dick Enberg noted in his introduction to one Miami game, "high-tech pro-style offenses" and players on both sides who were "destined for NFL glory." In fact, the FSU-Miami clashes of that era were the first time I can recall watching a college

---

9. "The guys of that era delighted in the fact that the administration was mortified of them," said *Miami Herald* columnist Dan Le Batard. "If they beat up the pizza guy, I'd get a call from one of them saying, 'We beat up the pizza guy.' They all thought it was funny that the administration was horrified by their existence and needed them all at once because of the publicity that they brought."

10. The next year, another Florida State kicker missed a game-tying field goal in the final seconds; Miami, however, lost in the national championship game that season to Alabama, proving once more that a sequel is never as good as the original, and long-anticipated NCAA sanctions finally descended on the program in late 1995.

game that *felt* so utterly professional: The execution, the speed, the talent level. And I lamented this at the time. I remember thinking that the state of Florida was blurring the line between college and pro so completely that in another twenty years we wouldn't be able to tell the difference.

But now I look back, and I see the choreography and show-manship, and I watch Miami's players swarming that field in the final seconds in a purposeful subversion of the NCAA's wishes, and I wonder if this civil disobedience was so utterly progressive that I can only fully appreciate it in retrospect.

VI.

"The rules didn't apply to them," Dan Le Batard, the *Miami Herald* columnist, once said of the Hurricanes. "They were not of the NCAA. It did not apply to them. . . . It was a complete disconnect."

And that was the thing about Wide Right I: It felt discon-nected from college football as we'd known it up to that point. I mean, you watch the highlights, and there's Miami's Coleman Bell making a remarkable catch, and then you realize that Bell was not even a wide receiver, but a backup tight end with little to no experience; or you look at Florida State's depth chart at quarter-back, which included, at that moment, both a future Super Bowl champion (Brad Johnson) and a future NBA point guard (Charlie Ward) as backups.[11]

---

11. Starter Casey Weldon wound up finishing second in the Heisman Trophy voting that year, behind Desmond Howard.

These kinds of things happen all the time in the twenty-first century, but back then, this collision of talent felt almost like a purposeful perversion of the amateur ideal, and it made it almost impossible to reconcile these kinds of teams with the notion that college football was a purely altruistic pursuit. And if it wasn't what we had long pretended it to be—if the evidence was right there in front of us, shimmying to "Me So Horny" in the end zone—then why should we pretend that it was?

"They want us to be like regular students," said tight end Randy Bethel, who admitted giving away money to younger players at Miami after he graduated. "But regular students don't generate revenue like we do. . . . I don't remember the last time that seventy thousand people packed into the Orange Bowl to watch a chemistry experiment."

VII.

Of course, they did some very stupid things at both Miami and SMU in the name of insurrection. They charged eight thousand dollars to an MCI phone card posted on the wall of a dormitory; they took steroids and carried unregistered handguns and siphoned gasoline from cars. They wrecked a sports car that had been purchased by boosters on their behalf. There were outright criminals tied in with the rebellion, but the cumulative effect of Miami's decade-long run of heresy was that we began to question the rules themselves. Why shouldn't nineteen-year-olds who score touchdowns be permitted a certain amount of unpremeditated self-indulgence? Wasn't breeding confidence in kids who came from broken homes, while also offering them an education, a fundamentally good thing? Why shouldn't we call into question the ethics of a system in which the central talent generates millions and receives no compensation?

Years later, when players and coaches were interviewed for ESPN documentaries about both SMU and Miami, they remained almost universally defiant. When it came down to it, they did nothing truly immoral, they said. The system was inherently at fault. Their purpose, they seemed to be saying, was to exact change, and they didn't have to apologize for flouting the rules in order to demonstrate the injustice of those rules.

The best thing Miami and SMU ever did was not win football games. Victory achieved by such radical methods is hollow on its own. The best thing Miami and SMU ever did was that they refused to say they were sorry for the way they won football games. And eventually, their lack of shame forced people to reconsider their ideals.

Faced with this insurgency, the NCAA and the assorted power brokers who monopolized the system had to do *something,* had to find a way to acknowledge that the product on the field had undergone a radical change, even if they weren't yet ready to undergo the fundamental change of bulldozing the system itself. The year after that Miami–Florida State game, they created the Bowl Coalition, a more sophisticated method of determining a national champion. It was a question the NCAA had actively avoided, since crowning a national champion would have been an admission that college football was enough of a zero-sum pursuit that things like national championships actually mattered. It turned out that the Bowl Coalition was a flawed solution, but it was progress; it took twenty years, but it eventually evolved into a four-team playoff system at the very moment that amateurism itself seemed imperiled by a series of courtroom challenges.

Would all of this be possible without the Hurricanes, and without games like Wide Right I, and without the audacity of men like Henry Lee Parker? Maybe. Perhaps it was an inevitable societal evolution, driven by a more sophisticated understanding of race and class two decades after the civil rights movement. It felt unsettling at the time, as militant ideas often do. But all this utter disregard for the existing structure of the sport in the eighties—the culminating shouts of *So what?*—helped us realize that maybe things could be better than they'd always been. In the end, the black hats turned out to be the good guys after all.

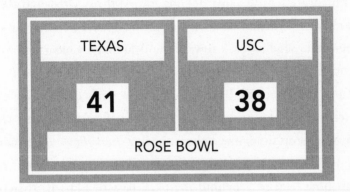

TEXAS	USC
41	38
ROSE BOWL	

January 4, 2006

The Ballad of Reggie Bush

Discussion Topics: Fresno State • *The Twilight Zone* • Todd Blackledge • The 1983 NFL Draft • Tecmo Bowl • EA Sports NCAA Football • Pete Carroll • Matt Leinart • Vince Young • The Iron Bowl • Jonathan Franzen • Tebow

I.

One of the most breathtaking displays of human physicality I have ever witnessed took place well after midnight, Eastern Standard Time, on a November night in 2005. I was at home, watching a college football game between the University of Southern California and Fresno State, and a USC running back named Reggie Bush cradled a handoff in the backfield, broke through the left side of the offensive line, and careened toward daylight. He sprinted twenty-five yards, angling toward the sideline, and then he ran out of room, and instead of giving up and stepping out of bounds, or angling back toward the field and a violent point of contact, Reggie Bush just *stopped*.

For a split second, Bush appeared to actively deliberate what direction to take next; it was almost as if he'd mustered the power to stop time, like a character in a *Twilight Zone* episode. And in that instant, with the football in his right hand, he somehow feigned a behind-the-back pass to himself, thereby freezing the three defenders directly in front of him. Then he cut across the field, outrunning every single person on it until he reached the end zone. He pointed a finger toward the sky, and the Los Angeles Memorial Coliseum shook, and Reggie Bush wound up with 513 all-purpose yards, and USC won the game, and three weeks later Bush was awarded the Heisman Trophy as the sport's player of the year.

I still think those eleven seconds comprise one of the greatest things I have ever witnessed on a football field. It's probably my favorite single play of all time that didn't involve any sort of premeditated emotional allegiance. I didn't really care if USC won or lost; I had no strong personal feelings about the Trojans' dynastic run in the mid-2000s, one way or another. But then Bush went ahead and reversed the time-space continuum, and it was so absurd that I stood and shouted and woke up my wife and probably half of my apartment building. I'm pretty sure I texted a friend of mine with nothing but a string of exclamation points, and then he texted me back with an even longer string of exclamation points, and then I rewound my DVR and watched it six more times.[1] It was the signature highlight of a career that would never be quite that amazing again.

That season marked the absolute peak of Bush's career. He was drafted with the second pick by the New Orleans Saints; he would eventually be stripped of his Heisman Trophy and retroactively cost USC a national championship for allegedly taking hundreds of thousands of dollars in gifts from sports agents. (According to the NCAA record books, that run against Fresno never actually happened. According to the Heisman Trophy Trust, there is no official winner of the 2005 award.) As I write this, he is preparing to play for his third NFL team, and while he is a serviceable (and occasionally very good) NFL player, it seems pretty clear that he will never be as good a professional running back as he was a college running back, because he was the greatest college running back of his generation.

By certain standards, Reggie Bush's career is a bust. And this will bother certain people more than it bothers me.

II.

My first favorite college football player was Todd Blackledge, the quarterback for Penn State's 1982 national championship team. Blackledge was from Canton, Ohio, the son of an NFL coach, six-foot-three, 225 pounds, a classic pocket passer with a strong arm and an unshakable aura and a wisp of a mustache. During his senior year, he led Penn State to a comeback win over Nebraska

---

1. In the process of formulating this sentence, I just watched it four more times on YouTube.

by driving the length of the field for a touchdown in seventy-four seconds. In the Sugar Bowl against Georgia, he threw a picturesque bomb along the sideline to a diving Gregg Garrity for the game-winning touchdown. That Penn State squad was the first national title team ever to gain more passing yards than rushing yards, belying the inherently conservative philosophy of their coach, Joe Paterno. Blackledge was versatile enough, and poised enough, that he altered the thinking of a coach who had been bred, like most midcentury football coaches, to believe that the forward pass was an unnecessary risk.

Todd Blackledge was, by all accounts, a solid citizen—he was the volunteer Big Brother to a kid on my Little League team, which boosted that kid's social status tenfold—and he seemed like he would have, at worst, a solid professional football career. He was drafted in the summer of '83 with the seventh overall pick by the Kansas City Chiefs, and in any other year Blackledge might have succeeded or failed on his own terms, but 1983 happened to be the Year of the Quarterback, and while Blackledge was drafted behind John Elway, he was also drafted ahead of two quarterbacks (Dan Marino and Jim Kelly) who would make the Pro Football Hall of Fame and two quarterbacks (Ken O'Brien and Tony Eason) who would have solid, if unspectacular, professional careers. Blackledge lasted five seasons, threw more interceptions than touchdown passes, retired, and became a low-key color commentator who may be best known for his appetite.[2]

---

2. Each week, Blackledge devours some kind of artery-clogging college town specialty for a segment called "Todd's Taste of the Town." I am biased, of course, but I do believe that, regardless of what you think of his football acumen, he is quite adept at conveying his enjoyment of oversized stuffed pancakes.

"I was surprised I was the second guy picked, I really was," he said in a recent ESPN documentary about the '83 draft. "I did consider myself to be a winner."

All of this was beyond his control. Blackledge was great, and he was a winner, and then, largely due to outside circumstances, he was (comparatively) not great at all, and he was (comparatively) not a winner. He was a prototypical college player, and an incompatible professional player; he was, by virtue of his graduation date, an all-time NFL draft bust. And this bothers certain people more than it bothers me.

III.

There was no single moment when the NFL eclipsed college football in popularity. It just kind of happened, the way many other (more significant) cultural changes took hold in America in the middle of the twentieth century. The closest thing to a watershed is probably the iconic 1958 Colts-Giants championship game, which ended with Alan Ameche's end-zone dive, but that predated the arrival of Pete Rozelle and the innovative television deals that brought professional football to the masses.

Up until then, though, pro football was a secondary pursuit. The college game was the only football that existed until the 1920s, and because it was intimately tied to the sentimental experience of college itself, it came across as a purer enterprise. Professional sports (with the exception of baseball, which was already shrouded in myth) were seamier; professional football often did not pay well enough or offer enough luster to lure the highest-profile players in the college game. And so you did your four years, you became a campus legend, and then you found a job at a local rubber company (like Jay Berwanger, the first Heisman Trophy winner, in 1935, who turned down the Bears' offer of a $13,500 salary) or you became a history teacher (Larry Kelley, Yale, winner of the 1936 Heisman) or an FBI agent (Davey O'Brien, TCU, winner of the 1938 Heisman, who actually did play two years in the NFL, led the league in several categories, and then retired and was assigned to a bureau field office in Missouri). "Pro football has never been able to sell itself completely to the fans who are so wild over the collegiate version of the sport," wrote *Sport* magazine in 1952. "Many people stubbornly insist upon regarding football as a rah-rah game which isn't the same when you take away the rah-rah."

Sixty years later, the NFL has so eclipsed every other sport in popularity that it seems unfair to compare it to anything else in America, let alone another sport. And yet people still do it, because it is only natural to do it, because college and pro are so obviously intertwined, because one leads to the next and because ideas trickle up from one to the other and because very often the best players in one do not prove to be the best players in the other. There are those who peak early and those who bloom late; there are behemoths from small schools who don't break out until they are placed into the backfield of the New York Giants, and there are high-profile skill-position players who never advance off the practice squad of the Jacksonville Jaguars. And because of this, there is a sense, among certain hard-core NFL fans, that college football is a trifle, a ground for training and experiment, a quaint rah-rah Saturday ritual that serves as a mere prelude to the real thing on Sunday afternoons.

And in a way, these people are being closed-minded and prejudicial. And in a way, they're completely right. And this bothers me more than it bothers certain people.

IV.

The genesis of reality-based football video games dates back to the 1980s, to the lineage of Tecmo Bowl and Super Tecmo Bowl, to Nintendo and Sega and on into the PlayStation/Xbox era, which is when I discovered the title that I've probably spent more hours playing than I have doing any single thing that's not directly related to my ongoing survival as a human being.

It began in the early 2000s, when my roommate brought home a PlayStation from his job. (I'm unsure how a writer for a music magazine managed to finagle a complimentary PlayStation, except that it was the early 2000s, and publicists are sometimes very desperate.) We were children of the Nintendo era; at first, we didn't know what to do with this advanced machine, other than stare at the controllers and express concern that they had "too many buttons." But then we realized that, every summer, EA Sports manufactured a hyperrealistic NCAA Football video game, with electronic avatars based on real-life college players (even though the makers of the game could not *admit* that these avatars were based on actual humans, since those actual humans were amateur athletes who could not be compensated for the use of their likenesses). And other than meeting our wives and witnessing terrorist attacks, this was, for us, the most meaningful moment in our thirties.

We have played every iteration of The Game since then, and we shall play it in whatever iteration exists in the future, if it exists at all. (As I write this, lawsuits have put The Game on hold, after accusing The Game's makers of profiting off the likenesses of the college students who were unable to share in the profits themselves; it was kind of a slam-dunk case, since The Game is revered for its "accurate" ratings of players, and since the most The Game would do to disguise its attempts to co-opt realism was randomly turn, say, a white kicker into a black dude with dreadlocks.) We have played The Game in person, and we have played The Game online. We have had long and in-depth and embarrassingly personal discussions about how The Game serves as a metaphor for our wants and our needs and our subconscious desires. We have evoked The Game as a metaphor when facing the major decisions of our adulthood; we have turned to our spouses for advice about The Game in the midst of long losing streaks.

The Game, of course, is wildly popular outside of our respective households. The Game is one of EA Sports' bestsellers, but it pales in comparison to EA's bestselling sports game of all, which is John Madden's NFL football simulacrum, which is essentially the same game, except it is based on National Football League teams (and the players receive a cut of the profits).

Except here's what we've found: It isn't the same game.

One year, my roommate[3] received a free copy of Madden in exchange for subscribing to a sports magazine. We tried it, and

---

3. Who is obviously no longer my roommate.

it was very much like The Game, but it was also subtly and fundamentally different. And because these sports games are now so deeply grounded in realism, Madden felt different in the exact way, at least to us, that college football feels less potent than professional football. Madden was more structured, more plodding; Madden had less variety and more straight-ahead plunges. Madden felt far less irreverent, far less replete with possibility, than The Game did. Madden is for hyperactive perfectionists, just like the NFL; The Game is for sentimental nostalgists who still believe in the flukish potential of the double reverse and the triple option. Madden felt far more like *work*,[4] which is a measure of how tangible and ultrarealistic sports games have become, but which also explains why my roommate and I never wound up playing it again.

V.

On the fourth evening of January in 2006, Reggie Bush and the USC Trojans played the Texas Longhorns in the Rose Bowl for the national championship, and what transpired might be one of the greatest pure college football games in the history of the sport. USC had won thirty-four consecutive games[5] under cheerful spir-

---

4. A few years ago, EA released a game called NFL Head Coach, which was essentially Madden without the actual gameplay. It involved all the labor of managing and coaching a professional sports franchise and none of the joy. At first, when this game came out, my roommate and I thought it might be amazing, but it got incredibly boring in short order. It proved universally unpopular.

5. A number of those wins would be vacated due largely to the alleged improprieties of Reggie Bush.

itualist Pete Carroll, an NFL flameout who seemed determined
to defy the draconian stereotype of the college football coach.
Carroll opened his practices to the media; Carroll was jolly and
upbeat and a total laid-back dude, and, according to a magazine
article by the writer J. R. Moehringer, Carroll spent his nights trying to broker peace among gang members in South Central. His
Trojans were a reflection of the SoCal ethos: They were glamorous
and likable and startlingly talented (and ultimately entwined with
corrupt influences). Led by Bush and heartthrob quarterback
Matt Leinart and a burly backup running back named LenDale
White, the Trojans' offense was *almost* an NFL offense as it was.

And on the other sideline: Texas, led by a quarterback named
Vince Young, a gregarious junior from a rough neighborhood in
Houston who may have been, up to that point, one of the five
greatest pure athletes ever to play the position. "The two most
explosive players in college football," color analyst Dan Fouts
called Young and Bush during the pregame. In the midst of a
single pedestrian run, he compared Bush to both Walter Payton
and Barry Sanders; when Bush tumbled head-over-heels into the
end zone while tiptoeing along the sideline for a key touchdown,
play-by-play man Keith Jackson mentioned that he'd passed Reggie Bush in a hallway earlier in the week and done nothing but
uttered the word "Wow." When Young rolled to his left, nearly fell
down, then cut back to his right to run for a touchdown that cut
the USC lead to 38–33 with four minutes to play, Fouts said, "I
tell you, Keith, I've never seen anybody like him in my life."

The game hinged on a fourth down and short, and White was
stuffed by the Texas defense, and then Young led his team downfield, and on a fourth-and-five at the USC nine-yard-line with

twenty-six seconds to play, Young scrambled to his right, charged toward the end zone, scored the game-winning touchdown, and vanished into a phalanx of photographers and sideline dwellers. It was, without question, the highlight of Vince Young's young life. Afterward, his professional career would spiral downward in a series of strange and tawdry incidents involving bouts of depression and photos of him standing shirtless in nightclubs.

To watch the 2006 Rose Bowl now is to realize that college football is its own unique entity. To watch the 2006 Rose Bowl is to understand that there are certain incompatibilities between college football and professional football that will never be fully understood, no matter how much money is poured into the science of scouting. Reggie Bush's NFL career has been okay, and Matt Leinart has become a backup quarterback who might be more famous as the guy who dated a reality television star. LenDale White packed on the pounds—one especially cruel NFL general manager, upon seeing White shirtless at the combine, claimed that he "needed a bra"—and flamed out of the league, and, as I write this, Vince Young is unable to hold down a position as a backup.

All the stars of the greatest national championship game of the twenty-first century have essentially been failures as professionals. And this only makes me love college football more.

VI.

I realize how college football must look from the outside. I realize that if alien replicants ever parachuted into, say, Birmingham,

Alabama, for the Auburn-Alabama Iron Bowl game, they would see all these clans shaped by geography and family history and, occasionally, by pure chance,[6] and they would see that all of this is embedded in supposed institutions of higher learning. They would see that these players are not professionals, but that they are treated as professionals, other than the fact that they do not explicitly get paid. They would witness an unabashed reverence for man-children who are not the best at what they do, but may someday be among the best, or may someday fade into obscurity as car dealers and construction managers and FBI agents. What can college sports possess, these replicants would wonder, that the professionals do not? Why not just spend the other half of the weekend watching a more polished brand of football? Isn't this like spending seventeen dollars to watch a student film at an IMAX theater, or spending $27.95 on an unpublished novel written by an MFA student instead of a hardcover copy of *The Corrections*? How can anyone possibly argue that an inherently inferior product is somehow superior?

---

6. When my friend Brant Rumble, the editor of this book, moved to Birmingham as a child, the first thing his classmates asked was not his name. They asked: *Auburn or Alabama?* The fact that the first word out of Brant's mouth was *Auburn* has shaped his entire existence as a human being. [EDITOR'S NOTE: "Well, my response to the question wasn't quite 'pure chance.' My dad went to Auburn, and had hung a poster of the 1982 Iron Bowl final scoreboard (with the Auburn students, after a 23–22 win, tearing down the goalpost in the foreground) above the headboard of my bed while we still lived in Atlanta (we moved to Birmingham in March 1983). I don't remember watching that 1982 Iron Bowl, but I might have been in the room. I didn't fully understand what it all meant, but I understood that Auburn was our preference; I was aware of the Auburn plaque my dad had hung in our main room; he had some Auburn sportswear. In late 1982, I watched part of Bear Bryant's final game at a friend's house in Atlanta, and I remember my friend's dad telling me that my dad would want me to pull for the other team. In other words, I'd been adequately prepped for the fateful question. What was more like chance was my dad's choice to go to Auburn in the first place, although I know he had his reasons for doing so."—Brant Rumble]

The reflexive rejoinder to this is to focus on the pageantry, on the atmosphere, on the tradition, on everything that surrounds the game rather than the game itself. And this is part of it; there is a sense of place inherent to college football that isn't the same in the pros.[7] College football happens, mostly, in small towns where nothing else is happening. There are live mascots and tailgates and the energy of thirty thousand undergraduates fueled by bladders of four-dollar vodka. The best professional football crowd, currently in Seattle, is equivalent to the sixth- or seventh-best Southeastern Conference crowd. Nobody watches, say, a Falcons-Panthers game for the atmosphere. They watch it for the occupational expertise.

But there's more to it than that, and I think it goes back to Todd Blackledge and Reggie Bush and Vince Young and hundreds of others like them, great college players with inherent weaknesses in their game. I think there's something beautiful about college football's imperfection, about the notion that the players themselves are works in progress, that they fall victim to corruption and excess, and sometimes they party with too much vigor (like a lot of us did in college),[8] that they do cocky things and they do stupid things and they sometimes lose games they have no

---

7. I also recognize that opposing worldviews are often based on upbringing: If you grew up in the Northeast, you were probably bred to care more about the NFL. If you grew up in the South, it's probably the opposite. If you grew up on the West Coast, you were probably too busy surfing and listening to *American Beauty* to care much either way.

8. I once got incredibly drunk on Sambuca, for reasons I can't recall, and went to a pizza place with a girl I was trying to woo, who happened to be friends with Penn State's starting quarterback, who happened to be future Super Bowl quarterback Kerry Collins. I remember Collins mocking me mercilessly, probably because I'd done the same thing to him in the student newspaper.

right to lose because they are too full of themselves to take their opponent seriously. They have weird throwing motions, and they run awkwardly, and they drop wide-open passes, and they fall in love with fake dead girlfriends; they are raw and young and they only have to get one foot inbounds instead of two and they give speeches that would sound idiotic in an actual workplace, but because this is college, and because that intangible spirit still persists, they become folk heroes.

VII.

I'm reluctant to even bring up Tim Tebow, but I'm not sure if I can write an essay about what college football means without mentioning Tim Tebow. And I know that Tebow is beloved for many reasons (largely among Christians and graduates of the University of Florida and Fox News anchors), and I know that he's hated for even more reasons (his open proselytizing and his ESPN-fueled overexposure foremost among them), but there may be no better example of a pure college football player in the modern era than Tebow, and I wonder if this gave professional football fans a reason to dislike him even more than they already did.

In 2008, after his Florida Gators suffered an early-season loss to Ole Miss, Tebow delivered an unbelievably earnest forty-second poetic soliloquy, with tears in his eyes, that ended with the promise "You will never see a team play harder than we will the rest of the season." Then he got up, blessed the room, and walked away.

Four months later, Florida won the national championship.

And this is how Tebow became a messianic presence at Florida, and this is why, when he emerged into the NFL, with his inaccurate arm and his staunch beliefs and his virginal persona, people presumed 1) this shit couldn't possibly be real, and 2) this kind of jingoistic absurdity might work in college, but it couldn't possibly work in the NFL, because the NFL is the real world. And so when Tebow started to win games as the quarterback of the Denver Broncos, and then won a playoff game, a raging anger built, and I think at least a small measure of this anger was based on the fact that the NFL is meant to be a reflection of the American workplace, a hard and unforgiving meritocracy that regresses toward the mean, and college football is a reflection of college, a place where we are marooned somewhere between childhood and the real world, a place where enthusiasm and emotion are very real parts of the game itself and are sometimes enough to overcome a flaw in one's throwing mechanics. And Tim Tebow, who was a marginal NFL talent with a collegiate persona, fit into one paradigm and did not fit into the other.

As an NFL quarterback, Tim Tebow was not destined to succeed. But does this make him a failure as a football player? At Florida, Tim Tebow is still a demigod; at Florida, they engraved a plaque with the words from his postgame speech, titled it *The Promise,* and hung it like a gospel.

VIII.

I don't want to make it seem like I hate the NFL, because I don't. I enjoy it immensely; I just don't enjoy it in the same way I enjoy college football. I like it when the NFL embraces college football concepts like the spread offense, but I prefer watching the way those concepts are stretched and manipulated more in the college game, because it offers greater possibility. And I recognize that it's probably *easier* to be a professional football fan, because while it is more brutal and mercenary than the college game, these players are choosing football as a profession, and they are being paid handsomely to risk their future ability to walk straight and think straight.

I am not naïve about the future of college football. I know the system is on the verge of change. I know that, within the next decade, college football will almost certainly veer further in the direction of professionalism. I know the pressure is building to dismantle the model of amateurism, and I know that amateurism is exploitative and cruel and inherently hypocritical, and the rationalist part of my brain is happy about this. I know amateurism is unfair, and I know it defies logic, and I know that it fosters corruption and that it works as a boondoggle for some cartoonishly self-absorbed people, like bowl chairmen and university presidents and Gary Danielson. I know that college football cannot continue to exist in its current form, that it has to evolve or it will become a regionalistic relic.

But I think what we're all afraid of—I think what makes otherwise intelligent and informed people hesitate at the thought of the NCAA opening the floodgates to free-market opportunities for its players—is that it will alter the fundamental character of college football. Because even if it is inherently the same, we want it to *feel* different. Because we don't want our relationships to players to seem commoditized, even if we know that they really are. Because we don't want it to seem like work, even if it is. Because we want it to be flawed and unpredictable. Because, at heart, the reason we prefer college football to the pros is that we are sentimental nostalgists, wishing we could retreat back to the time when we felt like maybe we had the potential to be great, too.

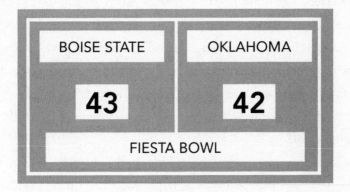

BOISE STATE	OKLAHOMA
43	**42**
FIESTA BOWL	

January 1, 2007

My Blue Heaven

Discussion Topics: The Hook-and-Ladder • The Statue of Liberty • *Strange but True Football Stories* • Georgia Tech 222, Cumberland 0 • Centre College 6, Harvard 0 • Utah • TCU • Chris Petersen • Georgia • LSU 9, Alabama 6 • Porcupine Saddles

I.

Here's a pleasurable thing I do sometimes, when I am despairing about the state of the universe: I go to YouTube, I search for highlights of the 2007 Fiesta Bowl, I run the video through to about seven or eight seconds, and I freeze the frame. At that point, I can see what's coming, and I can also witness the forces of nature driving things toward their inevitable conclusion. I can view the constellation of Oklahoma defenders lurching toward the top of the screen, attempting to defy physics and veer back in the other direction; I can see that a Boise State receiver has just caught a short pass on fourth-and-eighteen with under ten seconds left in the game and his team trailing by a touchdown, which makes no rational sense; and I can also see a second receiver circling around precisely five yards behind him in the opposite direction like a hungry wolf.

I can just observe the whole thing fixed right there in front of me, and even though I've watched it dozens of times, I can still say to myself, *There is no fucking way they're going to make a hook-and-lateral work on the final play of the game, are they?* Sometimes, I'll leave it there for several minutes and just stare. It is a hell of a stop-motion, like one of those great old *Sports Illustrated* panoramas of some iconic moment chronicled in midstream. And to my astonishment, every single time, when I press play again, Boise makes it work. The first receiver flips the ball to the second (lupine) receiver, and the second receiver's momentum carries him past the flailing Oklahoma defenders and along the sideline, and they tie the damn game. And then it gets even better: In overtime, trailing by a touchdown and facing another fourth-and-oblivion, Boise State executes a halfback pass for a touchdown, and then they go for two points and run a variation of an ancient gambit called the Statue of Liberty, the quarterback setting up to pass and then handing the ball off behind his back to win the game, 43–42.

Three sleight-of-hand plays, all of them in desperate situations, do-or-die, the upset of the century on the line. And every time I take in those roughly eighty-one seconds of highlights—the tension, the shock, the joy, the sheer absurdity—I ask myself, *What kind of person wouldn't want to see something like that happen again?*

II.

For much of my childhood, my favorite book was a compilation of gridiron odds and sods aimed at young adults called *Strange but True Football Stories*. If I am being honest, I probably hearken back to *Strange but True Football Stories* more often than any other football book I have ever read: Every time something weird and improbable occurs, I recall a chapter of *SBTFS* and recognize that the tropes of this sport are endlessly recyclable.

Chapter 2 of *Strange but True Football Stories* (written by Larry Fox) is entitled "When Disaster Struck Cumberland," and it tells the now century-old story of a team of young men from a small college in Lebanon, Tennessee. In the spring of 1916, the school received a letter from the football program at Georgia Institute of Technology, asking whether they might be interested in playing in Atlanta on October 7 of that year. Their reward: a five-hundred-dollar guarantee. As the recruitment rules were almost nonexistent back then, Cumberland's football manager, George E. Allen, endeavored to pick up several ringers from Vanderbilt University during a stopover in Nashville on the train ride down. But Allen was unaware that Vanderbilt had a big game coming up (I suppose Phil Steele's annual football preview magazine was not widely distributed yet), and three of Cumberland's players "got lost" in the city and never made it back to the train (which I think is young-adult-book parlance for "went on a bender"). The only recruit Allen could dredge up was a local newspaperman who played under an assumed name, because these were the days when newspapermen still had pride.

Cumberland made it to Atlanta with sixteen players, and used fourteen of them. Georgia Tech, under John Heisman, was about to commence a thirty-three-game winning streak. The Yellow-jackets led 63–0 after one quarter, and 126–0 at halftime. They gained 978 yards, and had thirteen different players score touch-downs. The final score was 222–0, but it could have been worse: The clock in the final two quarters was cut down to get it over with as quickly as possible. George E. Allen took his five hundred dollars and spent most of it "showing his players the sights of Atlanta" (which, I think, is young-adult-book parlance for "pissed it away on hooch and showgirls"). Eventually, Cumberland's Bull-dogs took the Pullman back to Lebanon, having set the standard for a hundred years' worth of early-season blowouts of under-manned programs. Many of them, including quarterback Charles Edwards, were reluctant to ever speak of it again.

III.

College football has never been very kind to the underdog, and I imagine some of this has to do with the fact that it is, and always has been, an unrepentant oligarchy.[1] It used to be that this oli-garchy was centered around geographic regions; now it's based on rough (and often nonsensical) geographic conflagrations of teams

---

1. "Dear Oligarch," a friend once opened a letter to Walter Camp. (True story.)

called conferences. Certain well-bred patrician conferences—the SEC, the Big Ten, the Pac-12, the Big 12—are "automatic qualifiers" for the major bowl games, and the rest, the dregs, the bourgeoisie, are "non-AQs." To elevate from one category to the other is perhaps the only way to ensure a lasting place in college football. But this is not easy to do, because the entrenched powers never want to give ground, and because non-AQs cannot play the same volume of quality opponents as AQs (which eliminates them from any kind of serious contention), and because when a non-AQ actually gets good, the incentive for an AQ to play them diminishes (which makes it even more difficult to prove that a non-AQ belongs). It becomes a circular debate: The AQs insist that the non-AQs aren't worthy because they "didn't play anyone," but they refuse to play the non-AQs themselves, because they aren't worthy of playing.

And yet it still happens that, every so often, a certain determined and enterprising school/coach manages to elevate a wayward program from the lower class. This has been true for decades, and it will remain true for as long as big-time college football offers both money and prestige to the schools that partake of it. And as proof, I refer you to chapter 15 of *Strange but True Football Stories*, which is titled "The Praying Colonels."

IV.

Chapter 15 of *SBTFS* takes us back to the cusp of the Roaring Twenties, to a place called Centre College, a private liberal arts school in Danville, Kentucky. Centre College had only three hundred students, and in 1919, several happened to be Texans, including a quarterback named Alvin "Bo" McMillin and a center named James "Red" Weaver. They matriculated to this tiny school based on a calculated decision by the school's alumni base; they came because Centre College was a distinguished institution that had produced two vice presidents and a Supreme Court justice and eight U.S. senators and ten governors and twenty college presidents, but Centre College had never produced an All-American football player, and some people who mattered wanted to change that.

So an alum named Robert "Chief" Myers was hired to coach the team, and he recruited five players he had led to an undefeated season the year before at a high school in Fort Worth, Texas, including McMillin and Weaver. Then he dispatched a letter throughout the state of Kentucky, which read, in part, "We want nice boys who are willing to take an anvil in each hand and fight a shark at the bottom of the ocean or ride a porcupine without a saddle."[2]

The pitch worked: Eventually, Myers got so busy with recruiting that he turned over the coaching duties to a former major-league baseball umpire named Charlie Moran, who was known as "Uncle Charlie." The story goes that during halftime of Centre's 1917 contest with Kentucky, Uncle Charlie delivered a stem-winder of a halftime speech that ended with a call for one of his boys to say a word of prayer. A lineman named Bob Mathias leapt up and fell into supplication, and Centre won the game

---

2. Was there an era when men in Tennessee rode porcupines *with* saddles? Let's just pretend there was.

3–0, and became known as the "Praying Colonels."[3] They went undefeated in 1917, and after the sport took a hiatus for a season so the country could fight World War I, the Colonels again went undefeated in 1919, and were invited to play the Harvard Crimson in 1920.

At that point, Harvard hadn't lost an intersectional contest in forty-four years, and they'd won the Rose Bowl the season before. They were the premier football program in the East, and since the balance of power was still concentrated in the East, Harvard was, at that moment, the standard that all other programs aspired to. They were the epitome not just of establishment academia, but of establishment football. In 1920, Centre managed a 14–14 tie with Harvard at halftime, and then they lost 31–14. When they arrived at Harvard for a rematch in 1921, the Crimson were in the midst of twenty-eight-game winning streak; the game was scoreless at halftime, and in the third quarter, Bo McMillin took a snap and sprinted to his right, until he was almost out of bounds, and then he switched directions, cutting back toward the other end of the field, reaching the ten-yard line and stopping dead near the other sideline. Two defenders surged past him, and McMillin scooted into the end zone, having covered something like a hundred and fifty yards in order to gain thirty-two.

It was the only score of the game. Centre won, 6–0. The firmament of eastern football had been cracked open, and the

---

3. An alternate story, forwarded by a sportswriter, goes that Centre earned the nickname by kneeling in prayer during halftime of a 1919 game against heavily favored West Virginia. At the time, they trailed 6–0; they scored two touchdowns to win 14–6.

game found new audiences nationwide. Centre 6, Harvard 0, was ranked in a 1950 Associated Press poll as the greatest football upset of the first half of the twentieth century. In the little town of Danville, they feted the team with an impromptu fire truck parade, and they painted "C-6, H-0" in whitewashed letters everywhere they could, in celebration of Bo McMillin's tricky little run to daylight.

A few years later, buried in expense and unable to keep up, Centre dropped out of the college football rat race. It was a hell of an underdog story, until everyone forgot that it ever happened.

V.

And this is how it happens, even today: An institution of higher learning decides it wants to be good at football, and so it commits resources to football, based on the theory that a successful football team can bring unprecedented publicity to a college, which broadens the pool of potential applicants, which raises the academic stature of the university. Is it a good thing? I don't know if it's a good thing. Theoretically, it *sounds* like a good thing, until it isn't, until corruption or apathy or other failures of will and/or ethics set in, and *Sports Illustrated* writes a cover exposé, and then it becomes an insidious thing and a shocking breach of morality and a symbol of the skewed priorities of the American bureaucracy because some five-star quarterback recruit from inner-city Atlanta accepted a five-hundred-dollar handshake from a local used-car dealer.

Usually, success at this gambit requires a visionary coach:

So it went with Miami under Howard Schnellenberger (and subsequently Jimmy Johnson) in the 1980s; so it went with Urban Meyer (and subsequently Kyle Whittingham) at Utah in the early 2000s, when the Utes jumped from non-AQ into the AQ Pac-12 Conference; so it went with the Texas Christian University Horned Frogs under Gary Patterson in the mid- to late 2000s, who landed a spot in the Big 12 Conference. All of these programs benefited from coaches who challenged the status quo, who opened up the playbook and devised new schemes and embraced radical thinking and flouted convention. And yet all of these successes engendered such irrational disregard from the fan bases of entrenched programs that they seemed to take it as a personal affront, as if it somehow cheapened their own place in the establishment.

I will admit, I was guilty of this dismissiveness in my younger years. In 1982, Penn State went 11-1 and Southern Methodist went 11-0-1, and nine-year-old self-interested me would have been appalled if the Mustangs had somehow stolen away the national championship, because clearly they were a secondary institution and did not deserve it the way Penn State did (in retrospect, SMU almost certainly had better pure talent; at the very least, they paid top dollar for it). I'm still not sure if BYU deserved to win the national title in 1984, after going undefeated while playing one of the weakest schedules in the country. I am constantly wrestling with the question of whether a team should be penalized due to forces beyond its control, and in no sport is this more relevant than college football, where the schedule is often completely out of anyone's control, where success depends on the clout of an athletic administration that can talk its way into a better conference or a home-and-home series against a higher-level opponent more than it does the actual results.

And yet it still works, as it did for Utah and TCU, as it did for Miami and BYU. You're an underdog, and then you win, and if you win enough or you win at the right moment then the establishment welcomes you into its wood-paneled club. It is a risk, and there are no guarantees, and there is always a chance that your school will be the one left waiting at the door.

VI.

Boise State was founded in the 1930s as an Episcopal junior college; it gained four-year status in 1965. The Broncos joined the NCAA in 1969, playing football in Division II, in an evocatively named conference called the Big Sky, and from there they slowly climbed the ladder, moving to Division I-AA in 1978 and winning a national championship two years later. In 1996, they went Division I, and started in the Big West Conference before sliding into the (slightly better) Western Athletic Conference, which is where coach Dan Hawkins won four league championships in five years before leaving for an ill-fated tenure at Colorado, depositing the Boise program into the hands of Chris Petersen, the mild-mannered offensive genius who coached the Broncos to the win over Oklahoma in the Fiesta Bowl. In his eight seasons at Boise, Petersen won nearly 90 percent of his games, and Boise regularly defeated Pac-12 and SEC and Big 12 opponents with bigger fan bases and considerably more resources, and yet even then, most people didn't seem to want to take them seriously.

I think there were reasons behind this. I've come to the conclusion that nothing Boise could have done, short of somehow sneaking into a power conference, would have ever elevated it to a level that the general population considers "elite."[4] I think the fact that the Broncos won that 2007 Fiesta Bowl on that series of trick plays led people to assume that their entire repertoire was based on sleight of hand, and not brute strength and raw talent, and this is something that certain football fans cannot abide. I think people presumed that a school from Idaho simply could not possess a similar level of football acumen to a team from, say, Georgia,[5] especially since their success came amid an era of SEC hegemony. I think people looked at Boise's crushing defeats, on missed field goals, to (very good) conference opponents in 2010 and 2011, and presumed this invalidated Chris Petersen's entire record. I think people saw a gimmicky program with gimmicky turfgrass engineers[6] and a gimmicky coach that still played in a gimmicky little conference (at the end of 2013, Petersen departed Boise and took the job at the University of Washington, thereby—

---

4. In his revisionist rankings for his TipTop25 website, poll historian James Vautravers actually bumped Boise down a spot from their No. 5 ranking in the Associated Press poll, behind a two-loss USC team. (Another retroactive pollster, Richard Billingsley, bumped the Broncos to fourth, behind three one-loss teams, including Louisville. Which I guess is about as much of a historical compliment as that Boise team is ever going to get.)

5. Never mind that the Broncos manhandled Georgia in the opening weekend of the 2011 season. I was there, and this was a road game for the Broncos, and they won 35–21, and it shouldn't have even been that close. They dominated a team that played for the SEC championship at the end of the season, and it was largely disregarded. Even before their loss on a last-second field goal to TCU that season, the Broncos weren't ranked higher than fifth.

6. To capture attention in their nascent years, the Broncos dyed their turf blue in order to stand out; that artistic statement, and a willingness to play games on weeknights in order to draw a national audience, actually seemed to work.

at least seemingly—closing yet another strange but true chapter of college football arcana). Still, I think Petersen's Boise State teams epitomized the modern underdog,[7] and while most people didn't mind the distraction, they would rather the Broncos now go the way of Centre College and vanish into the prairie like a strange dream.

VII.

In 2011, No. 2 Alabama played No. 1 LSU, and what resulted was a throwback of the worst kind, a fierce and frustrating defensive slog that wound up resolving nothing. Two Southeastern Conference teams, both undefeated, on a November night in Tuscaloosa; it was the highest-rated non-bowl telecast on CBS in more than twenty years, and it was resolved on a botched trick play and (literally) a game-winning punt. The final score was 9–6, and in the end, it didn't even matter who had the 9 and who had the 6. A couple of months later, Alabama and LSU would play each other again, this time with the national championship on the line, because what could be more fascinating than a rematch of a game that played out with such unsexy deliberation the first time around?

"The problem is that pairing the two best teams in a matchup is not as important, in my opinion, as producing the *fairest* matchup," wrote revisionist poll historian James Vautravers,

---

7. At the end of Boise's win over Oklahoma in the Fiesta Bowl, running back Ian Johnson proposed to his girlfriend on national television, which made the whole thing kind of a literal Cinderella story.

"which [in 2011] would and should have been LSU–Oklahoma State.[8] What we got instead was a relatively closed system. . . ."

But this is the thing about college football: I'm not sure anyone with any clout really *wants* a fully open system.

That 2011 season was Boise's best hope for national validation up to that point. And it's largely their own fault that they couldn't make it happen; the only path to a national championship for a member of the non-elite class is utter perfection, no losses at all. It doesn't matter how you lose, and it doesn't matter (generally) when you lose; there has to be a zero at the tail end of your record. And I think if Boise had made a last-second field goal against TCU in 2011 rather than missing it and losing their only game of the year, they might have wound up playing LSU for the national championship rather than Alabama. And I think if they made it through to the national championship, there is a strong possibility that, at the very least, they would have given LSU a better game than LSU gave Alabama. And I think it is not unfathomable to imagine that Boise could have defeated LSU and won the national championship, rendering any doubts about their national validity entirely moot.

At the same time, I also concur with the position that, in 2011—or in any other year—Alabama is objectively *better* than Boise State. I just wonder how relevant that stance should really be in the grand scheme of the capital-*A* Argument about playoffs

8. The Cowboys went 12-1 that season, with their lone blemish a 37–31 late November overtime loss to Iowa State that was mostly unfortunate because of its timing. If Oklahoma State had lost to Iowa State in September, they almost certainly would have been ranked No. 2 in the BCS, which is one of those vagaries of college football that no one's been able to properly explain except to say that's the way it's always been, and there's no real way to fix it. Teams just have to win when it arbitrarily matters most.

and national championships and bowl games and rankings. And I
guess this echoes another of those seminal questions that divides
college football fans: Do we care more about rewarding the best
teams, or about indulging our sense of possibility?

VIII.

Maybe, if you are the kind of fan who believes that the objective of
any postseason tournament should be to determine the *best* team
rather than the team that plays the best at any particular moment,[9]
you find it infuriating that this question is even a question. Maybe
you agree with what the otherwise cogent ESPN college basketball analyst (and Duke graduate) Jay Bilas said in 2013: *"Football
isn't based on Appalachian State beating Michigan a few years ago. . . .
Clearly people aren't pining for the upset the way we think they are."*

I think this is indicative of a general divide. I think there are
people like Jay Bilas, who just kind of presume that no one pines
for upsets, because this is not the framework from which they
emerged[10]; and there are people like me, who *do* pine for the upset,

---

9. Or if you are reading an aggregated version of this sentence in the *Birmingham
News*. In which case, I say, Roll Tide, and my home address is unlisted.

10. I'm really not trying to say Bilas is a snob; I'm just saying that maybe he doesn't see
things the way I do, because his job is to analyze in depth the upper echelon of college
basketball teams (which, interestingly, Duke was not, until the moment Bilas got there).
He is interested in seeing the best basketball, period. I enjoy well-played basketball, too,
but I am primarily interested in seeing whether strange things happen along the way,
especially when I can see that the individuals involved are at least *trying* to play well. To
me, the greatest thing to happen in college basketball in recent years is the emergence of
programs like Butler and Virginia Commonwealth as legitimate national title threats, and
that doesn't occur without the open possibilities of a sixty-four-team, single-elimination
postseason tournament that incorporates every conference in America (as basketball has).

who believe that upsets—or at least the constant and lingering possibility of an upset like Appalachian State's early-season shock at Michigan—are, in fact, the best thing about college sports. And this is what concerns me most, emotionally, about the impending four-team college football playoff, and about the lingering and uncertain future of the sport: That it will be entirely monopolized by the teams who are already established. That it will permit major-college football an excuse to further wall itself off from the underdog story, at a time when it is increasingly clear that the gap is narrowing, at least among mid-tier programs: In the first week of the 2013 season, eight Football Bowl Subdivision teams were defeated by teams from the Football Championship Subdivision, formerly known as Division I-AA.

I realize that, as it relates to the almost inevitable prospect of NCAA reform, this could be a good thing, because it will ensure that fewer institutions engage in the high-stakes big-time football gamble I noted above, and therefore don't get caught up in the bureaucratic shortcuts and compromises. And it's possible that I'm overreacting: It's possible that a four-team playoff could grow to eight teams by the time you read this, and it's possible that teams like Boise (and future Boises, whoever they may be) may eventually be able to schedule home-and-home series against a higher echelon of teams because those teams will be looking to bolster their nonconference resumes in order to qualify for said playoff. But it really does seem like a watershed moment. There's a possibility that Boise will be the last of its species, and I worry that if it is, we will omit something essential.

I recognize that it's a crapshoot, all this allowance for wild possibility. I recognize that sometimes—probably even most of the time—you might wind up with a team in a major bowl[11] that is worthy of the snobbish empirical judgment bestowed upon it. And this tends to fuel the prejudices of the closed-system establishment beau monde. But sometimes, it doesn't work that way. Sometimes, crazy shit happens, and hook-and-laterals actually come together like they do in practice, and the best team doesn't win at all, and it's bizarre and glorious and culminates in surprise marriage proposals. It's not that we're pining for the upset; it's that we're pining for possibility. Because if there are no more strange but true football stories, what's the point in watching?

---

11. Hawaii went 12-0 and then lost the 2008 Sugar Bowl to Georgia, 41–10; Northern Illinois went 12-1 and then lost the 2013 Orange Bowl to Florida State, 31–10.

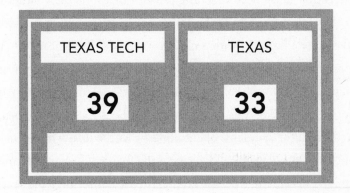

TEXAS TECH	TEXAS
39	**33**

November 1, 2008

Jokermen

Discussion Topics: University of South Carolina • Florida 30, Auburn 27 • Steve Superior • Banquet Beer • Ray Goof • Mack Brown • Stanford • The Fun 'n' Gun • The Air Raid • Four Verticals • Bart Simpson • Mike Leach • *Dementia Pigskin* • The Tortoise and the Hare • East Dillon High School • Texas A&M • Johnny Fucking Football

I.

One afternoon in the fall of 2012, Steve Spurrier held a press conference. He wore a scarlet golf shirt that clashed violently with the University of South Carolina's garnet backdrop; he opened the proceedings, as he often does, with an extended taffy-pull of the word *Ohhhkaaaay*.[1] What followed was not the weirdest media interaction of his head coaching career—that took place either in 2011, when he nearly broke into tears while upbraiding a local newspaper columnist with a rant that came off like a Second City improvisation; or in 1994, when he delivered a fifteen-minute Nixonian lecture about secret threats and enemies within the fourth estate. Nor was it a particularly boastful public appearance, given the standards of cheekiness that the man who refers to himself as the "Head Ball Coach"—the man who perfected trolling long before the Internet even existed—has set over the years. But there was one moment that stood out to me.

"We're doing something interesting that you guys may get a kick out of," Spurrier said, and he unfurled a Spurrierian smirk: His forehead crinkled and his head crooked and his chin seized up, forming a neat round cleft in the center. "Both of our punters are wearing number thirteen," he said. "Have you ever heard of that, Bart? We don't want the other team to know which one is in there."

I do not know who Bart[2] was, or why he was singled out for his knowledge of special-teams miscellany, but according to the video, it would seem Bart responded by raising a legitimate query about this unorthodox numerology, i.e., *What the hell brought this on?* And this gave Spurrier the opportunity to explicate. He talked about how one of his assistants had come up with the idea, and how maybe he'd make all his quarterbacks wear the same number,

---

1. Sometimes, the word is *Wahhllpp*. But the sentiment is the same.

2. Upon further review, my guess is that it was Bart Wright, the sports editor of the *Greenville News*. But it's also entirely possible that Spurrier had just decided to call every sportswriter "Bart" that day, just because he could.

too. I couldn't make out the next question, but I think someone asked how it might possibly be an advantage for Spurrier to play subterfuge with his punters, since they are both still just punters, and exchanging one punter for another is generally about as exciting as switching cell phone providers. How was this not trickery for trickery's sake?

And Spurrier, determined to justify his deception, said, "One kicks a little higher than the other one."

II.

In 1999, in his first and only season as the offensive coordinator at the University of Oklahoma, Mike Leach drew up a fake play-call sheet for the Texas game. It was just an idea, and he didn't expect it to actually work. According to Leach's book, *Swing Your Sword*, he and another assistant coach typed up the sheet, laminated it, and then gave it to an equipment manager. The equipment manager left it lying on the field before the game, underneath a bag of footballs that he later removed; a Texas assistant saw it on the grass, picked it up, and slipped it to the Longhorns' defensive coordinator, Carl Reese, who shoved it into his pocket.

"We just thought it would give them something else to think about," Leach wrote.

The second play on the fake call sheet was listed as DOUBLE REVERSE PASS. The Longhorns totally bought it. They overplayed the reverse on defense, and Oklahoma ran a crossing pattern underneath to a freshman wide receiver, who took it forty-four yards for a touchdown.

Twenty-nine seconds into the game, the Sooners had taken an early lead, based entirely on subversion.

III.

"Tricksters are hip's animating agents: the con men and hustlers, the fools and rascals, whom the culture invents to undermine its own rules. . . . What tricksters bring is enlightenment, not of absolutes but of the alleys around them."

—John Leland, *Hip: The History*

IV.

In 1966, as the integration of southern football loomed—as college football players began, for the first time, to openly question the authority of their coaches—Steve Spurrier made a brash and ultimately fortuitous power play. Spurrier, the son of a Presbyterian minister, was then the starting quarterback for the University of Florida. As a high school player, he'd drawn up his own schemes in the huddle, infuriating his coaches, until they started to realize that Spurrier's plays often worked better than their own.

In the first game of the season, a blowout victory over Northwestern, Spurrier—who was also Florida's punter—kicked two field goals, but he had since given way to a regular placekicker, and (according to lore) he hadn't even practiced field goals in weeks. Now the Gators were tied with Auburn, 27–27, and two minutes remained in the game, and their drive had stalled at the Tigers' thirty-yard line. Spurrier looked over at the sideline, into the eyes of head coach Ray Graves, and pointed at himself; as Graves was contemplating whether to send out his actual kicker, Spurrier apparently made the decision for him.[3] He put on a square-toed kicking shoe and booted a forty-yard field goal that won the game.

"He is a cool, articulate type with a campus reputation somewhere between Bobby Richardson and Superman," wrote Joe Durso, the *New York Times* reporter in attendance that day. A scout for the New York Giants compared Spurrier to Joe Namath; his own coach called him "the greatest clutch athlete I've ever seen." Auburn coach Shug Jordan, befuddled by the art of pronunciation, had inadvertently referred to him as "Steve Superior." A few weeks after Spurrier lived up to that accidental nickname, he won the Heisman Trophy.

"It wasn't that long," Spurrier said years later. "Most guys can kick forty."

I don't know if the Ball Coach was screwing around when he said that. I'm guessing he was, because that's what the Ball Coach does: He screws around. He once referred to himself as a "shit disturber." He takes pride in being the one football coach in America who *doesn't* subscribe to a theory of exhaustive workaholism. He admits that he didn't work hard enough to make

---

3. As with all things Spurrier, this is a matter of some dispute. Graves says Spurrier made the choice on his own; Spurrier says Graves told him to go kick it.

it as a professional quarterback; he throws his assistants out of the office if he sees them working too late. He plays copious amounts of golf. A few years ago, a photo of him hanging out shirtless at a NASCAR race, holding a can of Coors Banquet beer, made the rounds on the Internet.[4] He enjoys colorfully insulting reporters[5] and opposing programs[6] and rival fan bases[7] and his own players[8] to the point that it's hard to figure when he's actually being serious. His own wife called him a brat in a national magazine. He came of age in an era when college football coaches ruled with iron fists, and he seems almost actively determined to undermine the stereotype: Even when he is an asshole, he comes across as a theatrically ironic asshole. The best book written about him to date is a collection of his own quotes, in which he mocks Georgia coach Ray Goff (he called him "Ray Goof"), Florida State's Bobby Bowden, North Carolina's Mack Brown, the University of Tennessee, and pretty much the entire student body at Auburn.[9]

---

4. In 2013, another photo of a sunglassed Spurrier standing at a soda fountain in a fast-food restaurant, undone tie around his neck, giving the thumbs-up like a southern Keith Richards, also became a viral sensation.

5. After continued disputes with Ron Morris, the columnist at *The State* newspaper in Columbia, South Carolina, Spurrier insinuated that he was trying to get Morris fired.

6. Most famously in the 1990s, when after a scandal at Florida State involving free Foot Locker merchandise, Spurrier referred to the school as "Free Shoes University."

7. "We aren't LSU, and we aren't Alabama," Spurrier said in 2011, after a win over in-state rival Clemson. "But we sure ain't Clemson."

8. "I don't look at him as overly arrogant," former Gators quarterback Terry Dean once told *Sports Illustrated*. "Maybe egomaniacal."

9. After hearing that a dormitory fire at Auburn had destroyed twenty books, Spurrier said, "But the real tragedy was that fifteen hadn't been colored yet."

For years in the 1990s, his offensive plans defied the dull, cloud-of-dust template for winning that had largely defined college football up to that point: His scheme while coaching at Duke was known as Air Ball; given the dearth of talent he could recruit at a place like Duke, Air Ball served as an equalizer, a way for Spurrier to narrow the gap between his program and the others.

And when Spurrier made it work at Florida, at the highest levels of the sport, in the traditionally conservative Southeastern Conference—when this unapologetic passing offense won him a national championship—it undermined a generation of conventional wisdom.

Spurrier's playbook rebelled against everything Woody Hayes and Bo Schembechler and Bear Bryant and Darrell Royal believed in. It rebelled against more than a hundred years of orthodoxy, against the ideas that men like Walter Camp proscribed when they were arguing against the adoption of the forward pass in the early 1900s. He was not the only one pushing the boundaries—at BYU, Lavell Edwards had been throwing the ball like crazy all through the 1980s, and Miami won national championships with pro-style quarterbacks, and Bill Walsh had accelerated everything by devising the West Coast offense while at Stanford—but Spurrier was the most prominent executor yet of this rebellion on the college level. And just as important, he was also the most *stylish;* his personality conformed with the playbook. He sold his strategy right alongside himself. He became one of the highest-paid coaches in college football history before leaving for an errant turn with the Washington Redskins. He struck a blow against USC's student-body right, against Hayes's three yards and a cloud of dust, against the overused maxim, "Three things can happen when you pass, and two of them are bad."

This quote was such an apt summation of college football's overarching offensive philosophy that it has been attributed, at various times, to Royal *and* Bryant *and* Hayes; it's such an iron-fisted coach's cliché that any of them might have actually said it at one time or another. But Steve Spurrier, the petulant progenitor of a new breed of football coach, never would. When things went bad, when his quarterback made an errant choice, Steve Spurrier would hurl his visor to the ground like a petulant child, and he would berate his signal caller in public, and then he would tell him to get back out there and throw the damn thing again, until he got frustrated enough that he would send another quarterback out there and tell *him* to throw the damn thing some more. His offense was joyful and inconsistent and occasionally absurdist, to the point that it earned the nickname "Fun 'n' Gun." He called his quarterbacks "pitchers" and his receivers "catchers." He found alleys around the absolutes, and in so doing, in defying the stereotype of what a Head Ball Coach could be, he reanimated the game.

V.

Mike Leach was twenty-eight years old when he landed a job as an assistant at Iowa Wesleyan, an NAIA school coached by a gregarious maverick named Hal Mumme. Leach was a law school graduate and Jimmy Buffett enthusiast, ardently curious and intelligent. He got his first job as an assistant at Cal Poly, San Luis

Obispo, making three thousand dollars a year; he coached one season in Finland, where most of his team lit up cigarettes on the sideline. He spent those early years experimenting with philosophies, immersing himself in schemes. Neither he nor Mumme had a high-profile mentor; they viewed themselves as outsiders, subsisting on the fringe.

Mumme and Leach inherited a team that ran the single-wing, a formation that dated back decades, and had gone 0-10 the year before. They overhauled the entire scheme, drew up passing plays on restaurant napkins (sometimes they were cloth napkins, which didn't go over so well), and turned Iowa Wesleyan into a dynamic passing machine. They utilized the entire field, split their linemen wide to create running and throwing lanes, implemented crossing patterns that confused defenders, and gave their quarterback leeway to call his own plays at the line of scrimmage. In one game, he completed 61 of 86 passes.

Back then, they were still experimenting, still figuring out what worked and what didn't. They had seen what Spurrier was doing at Duke, his Air Ball offense, and Leach came up with the name "Air Raid." The moniker stuck; it became a brand. They left Iowa to coach at Valdosta State in Georgia, where one of their players' fathers would sound an air-raid siren every time the Blazers scored a touchdown, which was often enough that conference officials banned the noisemakers from the stadium.[10]

The signature play in the Air Raid is known as Four Verticals, and Four Verticals is exactly what it sounds like: In the backyard, it's called "everybody go deep." In video games, it is the currency

---

10. They eventually mounted it atop a nearby fraternity house.

of petulant twelve-year-olds with their fingers hovering over the X button. By practicing Four Verticals over and over again—by improving the timing and communication between quarterback and receiver so that each could read the other's rhythm—Leach and Mumme's Air Raid so perfected this play that it became almost impossible to stop. In 2008, when Leach was the head coach at Texas Tech, he ran it from the twenty-eight-yard line with eight seconds left, his team trailing No. 1 Texas by a single point, 33–32.

A classic football coach might have thrown short and set up for a field goal; Leach did not. His quarterback, Graham Harrell, rifled the ball along the right sideline to receiver Michael Crabtree, who caught it while the defender's back was turned, wrenched himself free, and skipped into the end zone for the game-winning touchdown.

Texas Tech ran Four Verticals eleven times against Texas. They completed nine, for 173 yards. More than any time in college football history, the playground came to life that night.

VI.

The concept of the "trickster" dates back centuries, to ancient mythology, to tales of deities and titans and shrewd coyotes who find ways to steal fire. A trickster, by the simplest definition, is a cunning or deceptive character who disobeys convention, but this can manifest itself in many ways. Bugs Bunny is a trickster; so is Bart Simpson. Bob Dylan is a trickster; so is Muhammad Ali. Tricksters are ubiquitous in African-American tradition: They find ways to manipulate language, to manipulate situations, to use wit and deceit to prevail over a stronger opponent. They are annoying and innovative and ultimately necessary.

For years, in the era of the authoritarian coach, the myth of the trickster didn't square with the overarching perception of college football: The torturous tales of Bear Bryant's training camps, the combat metaphors of Woody Hayes—the idea, as conveyed in a magazine called *Outing,* back in 1901, that

> [t]he manly qualities which are necessary to the building up of a successful player call forth the best class of college men, and the wholesome attributes which the game itself promotes are shown in the splendid examples of mental and physical manhood to be found among football men. This is true only if the game is played in the proper spirit.

So it went: Fifty years after those sentences were published, a journalist named Francis Wallace published a book called *Dementia Pigskin,* a Cold War paean to American football that warned that "a showy razzle-dazzle offense which leaves itself vulnerable" was the moral equivalent of socialism.

But times changed, and eventually the men who coached were forced to evolve with it. By the early 1980s, college football had become a burgeoning business, and small schools looking to sell their merits on the back of a successful football program were seeking unique thinkers.

"All of a sudden you have these places that had never won and were looking for something different," said another pass enthusiast, veteran college and NFL coach June Jones, in a 2013 interview with journalist Bruce Feldman. "They'd say 'We can't win the old-fashioned way.' . . . The correlation is you live by the pass and you get the run because you throw. Everybody else wants to run and get the pass because they run. With Hal, Mike and I the big similarity is the philosophy, 'Throw the football to get to the run.'"

In Leach's book, he repeatedly emphasizes that his offense is not based on trickery, that it is actually rather simple, that it relies on repetition and variation rather than outright deception. He likens his pass-heavy offense to the wishbone, the run-heavy scheme that Oklahoma and other heavyweight schools operated in the 1970s and 1980s. This is true, but it's also not true at all; by inverting the central philosophy of the sport, by throwing first rather than grounding his offense in the run, Mike Leach *was* engaging in trickery.

Here are two stories: The first, in the European, nontrickster tradition, is the classic tale of the tortoise and the hare. The tortoise wins the race, John Leland writes, "through his humble, steadfast virtue."

The second, an African-American slave tale, is about a terrapin who races a deer. The terrapin wins by positioning relatives who look like him at different stages of the course, while he waits at the finish line. "The deer," Leland writes, "is done in by his narrow belief system."

When Mike Leach was the offensive coordinator at the University of Kentucky, his teams went for it on fourth down forty times a year. That was nearly twice as many attempts as any other team in the Southeastern Conference.

"I've had the benefit of not having been institutionalized by the coaching caste system," Leach wrote, "and that lets me think my own way."

The trickster does not want to fight you toe-to-toe. The trickster wants to find the alley around you. The trickster wants to defeat you by challenging your fundamental beliefs.

VII.

"My first season at Florida was 1990. What surprised me was that the same mentality was still there: You gotta run the ball and play defense to win the SEC. . . . So I worked really hard not to act like those other coaches, especially how I talked. Coaches like to use the word 'great' all the time. I made it a point never to use that word."

—Steve Spurrier, to *ESPN the Magazine*

"The main playground for tricksters is language."

—John Leland

VIII.

The oddest sixty seconds in the history of the television show *Friday Night Lights* aired on November 4, 2009. A high school football coach named Eric Taylor—a character whose ideals were hammered out of our classical perception of what a great football coach should be—has stopped at a gas station and is eating some kind of unappetizing sandwich. He's just been forced out of fictional Texas powerhouse Dillon High and taken a job at a crosstown rival East Dillon; he's burdened by a lack of resources and talent, and he is facing a moment of reckoning when a crackpot who looks an awful lot like Mike Leach approaches his window and asks for directions to the city of Lubbock.

So Taylor gives the guy directions—is there no attendant at this gas station?—and the guy recognizes Coach Taylor, and here is where it gets strange, because I'm not sure who Mike Leach is supposed to actually be playing in this scene. Is he playing himself? Is he playing a Mike Leach doppelganger? Is he just a run-of-the-mill weirdo? Since Leach spent a decade as the head coach of Texas Tech, which is *in* Lubbock, you'd think he'd be able to locate it himself; since Taylor is, in this scenario, a high school football coach, you'd think he might recognize the most prominent college coach in the region if he approached him at a rural Exxon outpost to ask for directions. (I mean, wouldn't the real Mike Leach have recruited the fictional Tim Riggins?) So we have to assume this is some hyperfictionalized version of Mike Leach, a Mike Leach who lacks a job and a GPS and still keeps up with high school football minutiae enough to know that the fictional Eric Taylor is enduring an existential crisis in a tiny town in West Texas.

And so the fictional "Mike Leach" recognizes the fictional Eric Taylor, and launches into an inspirational soliloquy about Taylor losing "his inner pirate." This lasts approximately thirty seconds. Then he gets into his car and drives away. Eric Taylor sits there, holding his sandwich, looking thoroughly flummoxed.

The scene is never mentioned or referenced again.

*   *   *

"He's so different from every other football coach," Mike Leach's agent once said of him, "it's hard to understand how he's a coach."

This quote comes from a 2005 *New York Times Magazine* profile of Leach, written by Michael Lewis, that catapulted the coach from the fringe to the mainstream. Leach was weird and idiosyncratic and ironically cool; Leach brandished pirate swords in team meetings; Leach was the converse of all our traditional popular conceptions of the football coach. He was not a traditional prewar father figure like Knute Rockne; he was not a postwar martial didact like Woody Hayes. He was not an amalgam of all these traits like Eric Taylor. He was an oddball, advancing oddball ideas.

"A whisper of the old antipass bigotry [could] be heard in college football's conventional wisdom," Lewis wrote.

Soon after the story ran, Leach was profiled by *60 Minutes*. The ideas he and Mumme had devised in Iowa all those years ago—the concepts that built on Spurrier's concepts—would burst into the mainstream, buffeted by the fact that the men who devised them were just as counterintuitive as the schemes themselves. Leach's weirdness worked in his favor. He wasn't really drawing up plays in the dirt, but it kind of felt like he was.

By the early 2010s, offenses had become more spread out, fast moving, and pass-heavy; schools from smaller conferences, burdened by recruiting disadvantages, were throwing caution to the wind. Schools that hadn't won anything in years were finding ways to resurrect themselves. In 2012, Texas A&M joined the Southeastern Conference, the league that had captured every national championship from 2006 to date, the league that was still defined by defense and smash-mouth football and the throwback ethos that encouraged bigotry toward the passing game.

At the conference's annual media days that fall, in a spacious hotel ballroom in Birmingham, several incredulous southern newspaper reporters found alternative ways to ask A&M coach Kevin Sumlin—a disciple of Oklahoma coach Bob Stoops, who was a disciple of Spurrier and once hired Leach as his offensive coordinator—whether he truly believed he could *win* in the SEC by playing what they saw as gimmicky football, a hurry-up offense predicated on passing:

Q: What are your realistic expectations this year?
COACH SUMLIN: What are my realistic expectations this year? My realistic expectations are to win.

He said it, and then he said it again, and then he said it again. But no one in that ballroom, none of those reporters from Gadsden and Opelika and Chattanooga, actually believed he could do it.

IX.

And so into the breach, and into A&M's go-go offense, stepped a quarterback who had already earned the nickname of Johnny Football, a quarterback who had accounted for 160 touchdowns while in high school in a small Texas town called Kerrville, a quarterback who once put up eight in a single game. All of this had been brewing long before Johnny Football—whose real name was Johnny Manziel—won the starting job, a cocky redshirt freshman who had already posed for a police mug shot after a late-night brawl. All of this dated back to Steve Superior booting that field goal at Auburn, back to those wailing air-raid sirens in Georgia, building and proliferating as offenses spread and quickened and put up numbers previously unseen, as ten touchdowns in four quarters became a wholly attainable number to strive for. Johnny Football was just the vessel.

In November 2012, I went to Tuscaloosa to watch Johnny Football go up against Alabama. The Crimson Tide were the best program in the country; the Crimson Tide were undefeated up to that point; the Crimson Tide possessed one of the great defenses in the recent history of college football. The Crimson Tide's coach, Nick Saban, is a fastidious control freak who prefers to win by recruiting the best players in the South—hence, the best players in the country—and lining them up in classical formations. Alabama had won two of the last three national titles with speed and bulk and meticulous execution. Alabama did not need gimmicks to defeat you; Alabama would maul you if you fought them toe-to-toe.

So here was Johnny Football, facing a third-and-goal at the ten-yard line early in the game, a hundred thousand randy locals at Bryant-Denny Stadium screaming assorted niceties into his face. He took the snap, slid forward, bobbled the ball, somehow regained control, ducked out of a mess of bodies far bigger than his, scrambled left, and hurled a pass straight across his compact little frame to a wide-open receiver in the end zone.

A&M won the game, 29–24.

What tricksters bring is enlightenment of the alleys around absolutes.

In the short term, this game wound up meaning nothing. Alabama still played for the SEC Championship, and Alabama obliterated Notre Dame in the national championship game. But you could feel the establishment giving way. These offenses were no longer outliers, no longer gimmicks. These offenses were starting to feel more and more like the future of football.

A few weeks after Johnny Football defeated Alabama almost single-handedly, he became the first freshman ever to win the Heisman Trophy. His quarterback coach, a brash and enthusiastic thirty-three-year-old hipster named Kliff Kingsbury—who once played for Leach at Texas Tech—was soon hired in Lubbock as the new head coach. (Manziel spent the off-season partying with famous people, played one more spectacular season at A&M without winning an SEC title, and then turned pro.)

Leach lost his job at Texas Tech in 2009, after a dispute over his treatment of Adam James, the son of ESPN broadcaster Craig James. In his book, Leach insists that the firing was entirely political; he took a job at Washington State in 2012, where he attempted to breed success at one of the least successful major college programs in America.[11] At the same time, Spurrier was

---

11. In one of the first games I watched Leach coach at Washington State, his team led the University of Nevada, Las Vegas, 35–27, and possessed the ball late in the game. Instead of running the ball on first down, he threw deep. It's still kind of shocking—and a little bit thrilling—to see a coach defy the conservative orthodoxy like that, even though the pass was incomplete and UNLV got the ball back and nearly scored a potential game-tying touchdown.

winning at South Carolina with blue-chip recruits and a mostly run-heavy offense; the "Fun 'n' Gun," co-opted by so many others, was no longer his primary method of conveyance.

But by then, it hardly mattered. Their ideas had already flourished. The tricksters had undermined the culture; the tricksters had altered the language. The tortoise had become the terrapin.

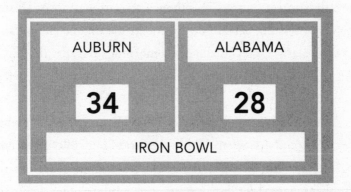

November 30, 2013

Get Behind Me, Saban

Discussion Topics: The Weather Channel • Oregon 0, Oregon State 0 (Toilet Bowl) • Oatmeal Creme Pies • Mick Jagger • Chip Kelly • Nepalese Carpeting • Stanford 17, Oregon 14 • The Play (Cal 25, Stanford 20) • Holy Shit • Holy Shit • *Chris! Davis!*

I.

An image I cannot shake: a Sunday morning in New Orleans, the day before the 2012 national championship game between Alabama and LSU, and the cabal that pulls college football's pursestrings holds one of those press conferences where the opposing coaches are forced to pose together in front of the championship trophy. It's awkward as hell, and if you listen real close, you can almost hear Nick Saban's teeth grinding in sync with the camera shutters. But then, a revelation of sorts: During the Q&A session, Saban informs the media that he and his wife set their alarm for six fifteen every morning, and that they lie in bed and watch the Weather Channel for thirty minutes before rising to greet the day.

This is the kind of thing we cannot help but talk about when we talk about Nick Saban. This is the sort of punctilious anecdote that defines him as a public figure.[1] I mean, who watches the Weather Channel for thirty consecutive minutes other than retirees, storm chasers, and control freaks? Nick Saban is the greatest coach in twenty-first-century college football, and maybe the greatest coach who ever lived, precisely because he is an unapologetically maniacal perfectionist; he is, as he has said hundreds of times, entirely "process-oriented," a "day-to-day guy," and a day-to-day guy doesn't leave the house without knowing for certain whether there is a warm front pushing across the southern plains. After making his initial confession, Saban joked that sometimes his wife spends that half hour in the morning lecturing him precisely on what he's doing wrong, both as a football coach and a human being, but I kept imagining him tuning her out and daydreaming of Oklahoma drills while the "Local on the 8s" music tinkles in the background.

One year later, the morning after Saban's Alabama team

---

1. A couple of years later, when someone lobbed Saban a softball question about whether he'd seen his own quarterback's picture on the cover of *Sports Illustrated*, Saban decried the reporter's superficiality by declaring that the only media he has time to consume is the Weather Channel. No one could possibly question his consistency.

embarrassed Notre Dame[2] to win his third national championship over the course of four seasons, I was again sitting in a hotel
ballroom, watching Saban summon yet another photograph
smile while posing with four different national championship
trophies. (I mean, the forcing of grins actually seems to cause
him physical pain, like a toddler opening up for the dentist.)
And in the midst of all this pretense, some young reporter asked
Saban a question that amounted to, *Why?* As in, *Why keep doing
this same job if you seem to have mastered it completely?* Also, *Why
so uptight, man?*

Saban stared down the questioner for a second, and then he
said this: "Why do you do what you do? Are you driven to be
the best at what you do?" And as his eyes bored into the deepest
recesses of the reporter's conscience, the reporter replied, "Yes, sir."

From there, Saban wound into a story that centered on an
old Martin Luther King sermon about a shoeshine man who
took pride in his work, and he said something about being the
best street sweeper you could be, and I think we got a little
glimpse of why the man, for all his ability to suck the oxygen
from a press conference, is one of the best living-room recruiters
who ever blew through the South. And I hurried back toward
my hotel room, all fired up to be the best damned street sweeper
I could be, just as soon as I stopped at Starbucks and checked
Twitter and Facebook and watched a few minutes of CNN and
ESPN and stared out at the pool seven stories below my window
and let another hour of my life pass me by without accomplish-

---

2. The combined scores of the 2012 and 2013 national championship games: Alabama 63, Notre Dame/LSU 14 (and those fourteen points were scored by the Irish
after they trailed 35–0 in the third quarter).

ing much of anything except the completion of the sentence you just read.

Such is the scuttled nature of my mind; such is the scuttled nature of modern life. Part of me is openly jealous of Nick Saban's near-sociopathic dedication to his craft, even as I fear that he might one day immolate a man in broad daylight in order to further his aims.[3] Ultimately, though, I recognize that the only thing Saban is actively seeking to vaporize is the inherently random nature of college football itself, the unpredictability and the forgetfulness and the short-attention span theater that results from hurling twenty-two college-aged kids—or for that matter, any human being whose brain has been warped by the constant disturbances of a twenty-first-century existence—into a violent arena in front of a national audience. He may be better at minimizing distraction than any coach who ever lived, but the great thing about college football is that even with Nick Saban in charge, the game fights like hell against any attempt at regimentation. In the end, just as it did at the very beginning, the game finds a way to set itself free.

II.

The first time I saw the University of Oregon play football, either live or on television—hell, the first time I became fully aware that the University of Oregon fielded a viable major-college football

---

3. Opposing coaches, only half joking, have been known to refer to Saban, in varied forms (for example, "Nicky Satan"), as the devil incarnate.

team—it was the second day of January in 1995. I had just graduated from Penn State, and I was fending off a throbbing hangover
in the end-zone seats of the Rose Bowl, watching the Nittany
Lions complete an undefeated season and lose the national championship at the same time. The sun set over the San Gabriel
Mountains, and the game never really felt close, even when it was.
I wore one of the seventeen L.L.Bean flannels that made up my
entire wardrobe at that juncture; the Ducks wore electric pants
and emerald jerseys and helmets that appeared to have been slath-
ered with honey-mustard sauce. Their uniforms stood out even
then, a thumb in the eye of their region's grungy ethos, as if they'd
been contrived by a flamboyant Hollywood costume designer for
the sequel to *The Program*[4] that nobody awaited.

The Ducks lost that game 38–20, and the next year they got
throttled 38–6 in the Cotton Bowl by Colorado, and after that,
I just kind of assumed they'd recede into the landscape, into the
vacuum that was college football in the state of Oregon, into the
dense forest of ignominy that had once produced the worst rivalry
game in the history of the sport: In 1983, in a driving rainstorm,
Oregon and Oregon State turned the ball over eleven times,
missed four field goals, and tied 0–0. (The game is referred to, in
local lore, as the Toilet Bowl.)

It's hard to fathom those games took place only a couple of

---

4. *The Program* was a preachy 1993 James Caan film about college football that's
most memorable for a moment when the star quarterback (and eventually several
other players) lie down along the center line of a highway. That scene was cut from
the film after at least one person was killed attempting to imitate it, and several others were nearly killed, including my college friend B.J., who would often get drunk,
rush just beyond the parked cars on College Avenue, and lie flat, shouting, "WHAT
MOVIE IS THIS?"

decades ago; it's astounding to think that those Teletubbies Oregon teams bear any relation to the metallic blur that, within less than twenty years, would become one of the most fascinating college football programs in America. What Oregon did over the course of those two decades, constructing an abruptly successful football program entirely through the power of modern marketing—and largely behind the fortune of a single benefactor, Nike CEO Phil Knight—is the most audacious and the most purely capitalistic experiment in modern sports. (Even now, I'm not sure if I should admire it or fear it.)

Other programs have attempted to elbow their way into the upper echelon of college football, but never with the sheen and panache and glitz of Oregon. As of 2014, the Ducks have not played a single game against Alabama, which is astounding, since they are the two highest-profile programs of their era: Both were ranked in the preseason top five every year from 2011 to 2013,[5] and the Tide and Ducks appeared to be on a national-championship collision course midway through each of the last two of those seasons. Set them alongside each other, a nouveau riche Pacific coast clan of garishly dressed blue-state speedsters versus an institutional monarchy of crimson-clad conservative southerners, and it feels almost Gatsbyesque. So it goes in college football; it is a world in which everyone at the top is striving to transcend their circumstances, to engineer their own luck. But this is the inherent danger of investing in a sport so tenuous, a sport where one loss can knock you out of the upper echelon, a

---

5. Prior to that, Alabama won the 2009 national championship, and Oregon played for the title at the end of the 2010 season.

sport whose practitioners are so tantalizingly young. Sometimes, insane shit happens, and there's not a damn thing you can do to control it.

III.

Let us take a moment here to celebrate the roots of Nick Saban's austere brilliance: This is a man who grew up in rural West Virginia, in the heart of coal country, whose father (Big Nick) ran a combination service station/Dairy Queen. This is a man who once, after he landed a D for refusing to get up and sing during a high school music class, was dragged by Big Nick 550 yards down into a mine shaft and told, *If you don't get a college education, this is where you're going to end up every day.* When he was eleven, Saban said, he started working at the service station; he cleaned windows, he checked oil, he gauged the tires, and he washed cars. He especially hated the blue and the black ones, because if his dad found a single streak, he'd make him start over again. "That sort of perfectionist type of attitude that my parents instilled in me," he said, "that's probably still the foundation of the program we have right now."

This is where Nick Saban came from, and this is where he's coming from. He is a serious man who does not tolerate unserious men.[6] He once told a friend that winning a national championship had gotten on his nerves since it fucked up his

---

6. As I was writing this essay, a video of Saban doing the Electric Slide surfaced on the Internet. Even then, the look on his face is one of maniacal focus.

recruiting calendar by a week. For convenience, he famously rigged the door to his office so that it shuts by remote control, completely oblivious to the notion that this is exactly what a cartoon supervillain would do. When *GQ* reporter Warren St. John, riding in a car with Saban, repeated a line his daughter had uttered about Mick Jagger's inability to hold a tune, Saban snapped back, "Mick Jagger *can* sing. Mick Jagger is a great entertainer." His lone vice, best as we know, is the consumption of two Little Debbie Oatmeal Crème Pies every morning for breakfast.

Saban came to Alabama in 2007 after the only true failure of his career, a short stint with the NFL's Miami Dolphins. Before that, he'd coached under Bill Belichick, and he'd rebuilt the program at Michigan State, and he'd won a national championship at LSU. When he got to Tuscaloosa, the program was still haunted by the shadow of Bear Bryant, a coach who had died nearly twenty-five years before. Whereas the Bear stood distant but oozed charisma, Saban is directed almost entirely inward. Even the Alabama fan base, the most zealous[7] in college football, treats Saban with a wary and distant curiosity; when Warren St. John (an Alabama alum) mentioned to a Crimson Tide fan whom he knew that he was going in search of evidence of Saban's humanity, he was told, "There's circumstantial evidence, but no proof."

This is what Nick Saban brought to Alabama: the idea that process trumps personality. Alabama wins because it recruits bet-

---

7. And occasionally overzealous: Bama fan Harvey Updyke became infamous in 2011 after he poisoned the trees at archrival Auburn's Toomer's Corner, then called radio talk-show host Paul Finebaum to brag about it.

ter players, and then trains those players to minimize the risk of defeat. At this, Saban's Crimson Tide are more efficient than any college team, ever.

In fact, the shadow of Saban's comprehensive micromanagement looms so large that it's already shaded into its own branch of myth: There was a report, the day of the 2012 national championship game in Miami, that Saban had ESPN removed from the televisions at the team hotel to avoid the chatter of the talking heads. I asked Alabama lineman Barrett Jones about this in the locker room afterward, and he assured me it was utterly false. But it spread because it *seemed* plausible. It is, after all, those small details that Saban notices that set him apart. "He's full of little things," Jones said. More than any coach who ever lived, he appeared to have prepared for everything.

IV.

After that Rose Bowl loss to Penn State, Oregon officials began to have discussions about improving the football program as a method of promoting the university. After a loss in the Cotton Bowl the next season, before those same officials even flew back from Dallas, they met with Phil Knight, who promised he would give his alma mater everything it needed to achieve sustained success, including a thorough rebranding. Hence: the endless garish uniform iterations that started cropping up in the early 2000s, along with the massive billboard of quarterback Joey Harrington that went up in midtown Manhattan, along with the late-night airtime purchased on the YES Network in

New York City so northeastern recruits could watch a tape-delayed broadcast of a team they would have otherwise never seen, along with the eventual adoption of a short-attention span offensive philosophy, under Coach Chip Kelly, that embraced tempo and speed and is engineered for chaos. And, of course, there was the money: more than $300 million from Knight himself, which included money for a library renovation and a law center, but much of which went straight into football, into a stadium expansion and an athlete tutoring center and most recently, the (at least) $68 million Hatfield-Dowlin Complex, a Versailles replete with Nepalese rugs and a duck pond and a barbershop with utensils from Milan.

As the dollars poured in, as their closet of "alternate" uniforms expanded into the dozens,[8] the Ducks got better and better. They recruited nationwide, stole athletes from California and Texas, found a quarterback out in Hawaii; in 2011, they came a few plays away from winning the national championship over Auburn. In search of something to differentiate themselves beyond the uniforms, they'd unearthed Kelly, who was, until 2007, a largely unknown offensive coordinator at the University of New Hampshire. Kelly's system, his hurry-up offense, his use of pop-culture-laden placards to signal his plays from the sideline, his low-key intellectualism—all of it seemed deliberately progressive, a shake-up, a way to both market his

---

8. "It's probably the easiest way for Oregon to cut through the clutter of college football, to be undeniably known for *something*," Paul Swangard, managing director of the university's Warsaw Sports Marketing Center, told writer Michael Kruse. "If no one knows your product exists, there is no demand for your product, and at the end of the day it's about 18-year-old kids. The uniforms are the key ingredient to getting those bodies there, and the bodies are what win you football games."

program and improve it at the same time. It revolutionized offensive football.

And yet, for all this investment (both in dollars and intellectual capital), Oregon could not overcome bad fortune. In 2012, with a national championship berth within their grasp, with a team that had put up at least forty-two points in its first ten games, the Ducks lost to Stanford, 17–14, in overtime, in a game that could have gone either way. Kelly, perhaps sensing some fatal flaw in his own system (at least at the college level), left for the Philadelphia Eagles, to coach professionals who embrace repetition and precision as part of their vocation.[9] In 2013, again undefeated, again on track for the national championship game under new coach Mark Helfrich (who maintained Kelly's offensive system), the Ducks fell into a deep hole early, came back to make it close, but *again* lost to Stanford, a physical team with a strong defense that plays a lot like an Alabama of the west.

All that investment, all that effort, all those recruiting coups and facilities upgrades, and Oregon was still victimized by a single nemesis, still subject to the random cruelty of a high-octane offense that occasionally gets tripped up by its own chaos, still borne back ceaselessly into its own past.

As of 2014, the Ducks and their benefactors have spent upwards of half a billion dollars, and have yet to win a national championship.

---

9. In the NFL, randomness and luck are not absent, but the discussion of them is certainly less prevalent than it is in college. For obvious reasons—more games, more practice time, more skilled practitioners—it's a more regimented product.

V.

The most utterly random sequence in the history of college football—the most unforeseeable single moment in the history of American sports—is the final play of the Cal-Stanford game in 1982. Trailing 20–19 after a heroic go-ahead field goal drive by Stanford quarterback John Elway, Cal received the kickoff with four seconds remaining, lateraled the ball five times, and reached the end zone as the Stanford band charged onto the field. The same guy who originally received the kick, Kevin Moen, weaved through the band and wound up scoring the touchdown, plowing over a trombone player while doing so. That play is now known as The Play, because it needs no further embellishment; it is such a wondrous thirty-second encapsulation of the screwball nature of college football that even the trombone player (Gary Tyrrell) has achieved a measure of immortality.[10] There have been other Cal-Stanford-*like* plays in both pro football and small-college football, but none is as patently absurd as Cal-Stanford, and none ever will be.

For a long time, I presumed nothing in my lifetime would ever top Cal-Stanford. For a long time, I imagined that Cal-Stanford would forever stand as the zenith of college football's ability to surprise.

And then came the Iron Bowl.

Jesus. The Iron Bowl.

---

10. "When I'm introduced to someone new and the person doing the introducing says I was the trombone player in The Play, there's recognition all around the world," Tyrrell told the *Daily Californian* in 2012. "Wherever I might be, they remember that play."

VI.

I will admit, when I first saw it, I thought the kick was going to be good. I was in a living room with five other adults, and ferocious in-state rivals Alabama and Auburn were tied at 28, and the officials had just put one second back on the clock to afford Alabama the chance to attempt a game-winning kick, and the Tide had already won two straight national titles coming into 2013 and were undefeated again and looked even more imperturbable than they had in previous years. So we all thought the damned thing was going to be good, and we continued to think so for multiple seconds, and part of that was the camera angle, the view from the end zone, the lack of depth perception inherent to watching field goal attempts on a flat-screen television, but mostly we thought the kick was good because of the man who chose to kick it.

That's how thoroughly Nick Saban's compulsive bent had wormed its way into our psyche by then: We just presumed that he had gamed this situation to the millimeter, that the kicker he trotted out to attempt a fifty-seven-yarder routinely made clutch practice-ending kicks from seventy-seven yards with a Mastodon album playing on Klipsch speakers four feet away and a student manager blowing an airhorn in his face. This is the same man who formulated an extensive contingency plan just in case his team ever faced a lightning delay; surely, he had this scenario covered in some laminated binder filed in an underground vault under the letter *K*.

So I thought the kick was good, and that's pretty much all I was thinking, and when it turned out it didn't have the distance and it landed in the arms of an Auburn defensive back named Chris Davis, I wasn't really thinking anything at all, because I was too busy screaming. Davis returned the ball upfield and along the sideline (a perfectly legal move on a missed field goal) and no one touched him; he outran the holder and outran some huffing offensive linemen and he scored the most holy-shit touchdown in the long history of holy-shit touchdowns.[11] I was in that living room with those five full-grown adults and two children, and the adults were all screaming, *Holy shit,* and the kids were sitting there placidly, staring at the television screen and grinning and relishing that rare instant when the adults became the children.

I imagine you might have had a similar experience on that particular Saturday night, if you happened to be in front of a television set for the climax of the Auburn-Alabama game. (After it happened, a whole subculture of YouTube videos of people *reacting* to the last play popped up, which led me to wonder if more people than I realize either 1) take the time to stage moments like these using their DVRs and iPhones, or 2) are insane enough to maintain twenty-four-hour surveillance on their own living rooms.) I cannot think of a single play in any sporting event I've ever watched that so completely traversed the spectrum of emotion from one pole to the other. It defied logic, and it defied common sense, and all the immediate talk about whether it was the

---

11. The best part of the live CBS call is play-by-play man Verne Lundquist simply enunciating his first and last name—*Chris! Davis!*—as he crosses the goal line. (A moment later, Lundquist calls it "an answered prayer," which feels, in retrospect, like the wrong way to characterize this moment; I love Verne, but no one watched that field goal soar through the air and beseeched some higher being for the kick to fall short, and for Davis to catch it and sprint past everyone on the field for a touchdown. No major-college game in history had *ever* ended that way. It's so improbable that it's beyond prayer.)

greatest finish of any game ever (which happens so often in this age of immediacy that it's often hard to tell if those claims carry any weight) tends to ignore the context of what made it so surprising in the first place, which is that it happened to a man whose legacy is grounded in the idea that he has a contingency plan for every situation.

Cal-Stanford was a break in the fabric of reality that will never be replicated, and Doug Flutie's last-second Hail Mary to lead Boston College over Miami was a Catholic prayer, and Boise State–Oklahoma was a Disney fairy tale. These things happen every so often, and sometimes they even happen more than seems humanly viable: Two weeks prior to the Iron Bowl, Auburn had beaten Georgia on a fourth-and-eighteen tipped Hail Mary pass in the final minute.[12] But *this* play, because it happened to Nick Saban, because it happened to the one man who seemed to have succeeded in wrangling spontaneity, tying its hands, and locking it in a basement with no food or water . . . this play is the most surprising sequence in the history of college football.

VII.

And I suppose that's the overarching idea I'm trying to communicate here, and I suppose this is at least part of what I mean when I've tried to explain, throughout the previous dozen chapters, why college football is fundamentally different than every other sport.

---

12. It almost doesn't matter that Auburn lost the national championship game to Florida State on a last-minute drive; in twenty years, the Tigers' two-loss season will be infinitely more memorable than Florida State's undefeated season.

In the end, it reverts back to the beginning. This is a pastime that was born as a spontaneous exercise on the grassy courtyards of the Ivy League, the brainchild of restless undergraduates seeking to blow off steam by barking each other's shins and throwing punches. And even now, 150 years later, as it is industrialized and corporatized and rendered in Technicolor at places like Oregon, as it is commanded and controlled and repressed by scrupulous men like Nick Saban, it is still ultimately untamable. There are those who seek to maintain control over the beast, and there are those who wish to set it free. Eventually, the adults give way to the children, and all we can do is watch.

AN EPILOGUE

January 2, 1987

The Grand Experiment

Discussion Topics: Penn State 24, Notre Dame 21 • University of Chicago Maroons • Amos Alonzo Stagg • Red Grange • Oberlin • Joe Paterno • Beaver Canyon • The Author • Despite His Doubts • Reasserting College Football as a Force That Gives Us Meaning

I.

In November 1990, four days shy of my eighteenth birthday, a strange and familiar ritual took place in my hometown. Five hundred miles away, a freshman kicker swung his leg, driving a football through a pair of goalposts, thereby completing Penn State's 24–21 upset of the top-ranked Notre Dame Fighting Irish. And back home, no more than a half mile from the freshman dorm room where I resided, a joyous mob crashed through a construction fence and into Penn State's empty football stadium, absconding with the goalpost from the south end zone.

Word spread fast, and an army twelve hundred strong formed around (and occasionally atop) the goalpost, and over the course of four hours, they marched in a spontaneous parade that lurched from one campus landmark to another, leaving behind pieces of the goalpost at each site like public offerings. They deposited a segment on the steps of the administration building known as Old Main, and they left behind a fragment next to the limestone shrine of the school's mascot, the Nittany Lion, and then they turned toward an idyllic neighborhood called College Heights and marched on the home of the head football coach, Joseph Vincent Paterno of McKee Street, whose address and telephone number had long been listed in the local phone book. And as if engaging in some final act of Holy Communion, they serenaded Paterno's wife, Sue, and deposited a section of the upright on the Paternos' front lawn.

"This," one senior told the student newspaper, "is the first time we felt like true Penn Staters."

I admit that all of this only seems weird to me in retrospect, on the far side of the worst scandal in modern sports history. We engaged in these kinds of impromptu conventions all the time at Penn State; we were always gathering in public places to celebrate one thing or another (or on occasion, to celebrate nothing at all).

We were always devising new ways to declare our fidelity to the place, and to celebrate our youth, and to congratulate each other for making such a wise choice of college, and to pay tribute to the football team that served as our public face. And only recently did I start to ask myself why.

II.

On Thanksgiving Day in 1905, the University of Chicago hosted a football game against Michigan, and tickets were almost impossible to find; at least one student was arrested for what may have been a primordial attempt at scalping. It was an occasion with enough pomp that women were permitted into the men's dorm rooms for pregame parties. After Chicago's 2–0 upset victory,[1] students set bonfires that lasted for days; they marched on the house of university president William Rainey Harper, who was dying of cancer, and sang the alma mater to him.

Harper, a onetime Yale professor, was the one who brought football to Chicago. Harper was the one who imported the Walter Camp ideal of marrying academics and athletics from back east; Harper, a former seminary instructor, was the one who believed that football could become a secular evangelical tool, that it could help establish the reputation of a fledgling university founded with Rockefeller money in 1892. (One professor called Harper "the P. T. Barnum of education.") It was Harper's decision to

---

1. Years later, Dennison Clark, the Michigan player who caught a punt near the goal line and was tackled in the end zone for a safety, committed suicide.

hire Amos Alonzo Stagg, a Yale graduate and Camp disciple who would, in the ensuing decades, become the model of the institutional football coach.

Stagg, ostensibly hired to run the school's physical education department, was the first football coach to be granted tenure. He made more money than the heads of the departments of philosophy and psychology. "His rugged honesty, his regard for truth, and his simplicity in life and manner have made him beloved of all who associated with him," the *Chicago Tribune* wrote of Stagg. "One could not fail to notice his home life, for that of no man could be more beautiful."

In his forties, Stagg was already referred to as "the Old Man"; he became one of college football's defining figures as it continued its slow expansion from the Ivy League westward. His Maroons went undefeated in 1913, and as his success carried on through the mid-1920s, he raised millions for the university through his mere presence. He was, for nearly forty years, the public face of the University of Chicago, so much so that it was often referred to as "Stagg's University."

And then one day, he was fired.

III.

I went to college at Penn State because it was everything I knew. We lived in suburban New York City until the summer of 1978, and when I was five, my father, a chemistry professor, took a job in rural central Pennsylvania and never left. The university was always right there with us, all over town, all across town, in signs and banners and on radio and television, its overarching presence built into the name of the town itself: *State College*. In high school, we were the Little Lions. There was no way to extricate the happenings at our school from the happenings at the university, and the happenings at the university centered around football.

This had been true since the late 1960s, when Joe Paterno, a graduate of Brown and a native of Brooklyn and a student of the Greek classics, took over the football program from Rip Engle (for whom he'd served as an assistant) and quickly elevated it to national status. At the onset of his tenure, Paterno, chaste and outspoken, sold himself through the concept he referred to as the "Grand Experiment," which would attempt to reconcile academic and athletic prowess in ways that seemed to defy a century-long movement toward the professionalization of college football. He gave a lofty commencement speech at Penn State in 1973, an address that spoke of "moral responsibility," and in its aftermath, began the process of propelling the university, a public college with a decidedly mixed academic standing, into a more reputable institution. Joe Paterno and his wife lent their names to a campaign to expand the university library. Joe Paterno raised millions for Penn State, simply by showing up at fund-raisers and rubber-chicken alumni dinners in Scranton and Allentown, and Joe Paterno elevated the stature of the university merely by espousing the tenets of the Grand Experiment far and wide.

He was the face of Penn State: His likeness was reproduced on coffee cups and on life-size cardboard cutouts and on rubber Halloween masks. The deli at the student union named a sub after him ("The Joegie"); at the stadium, students young enough to be his great-grandchildren chanted his name in rhythm ("JOE-PA

TER-NO"). When I mentioned Penn State to people who knew nothing else about it, they invariably said something about Joe Paterno (usually about his integrity, or about his glasses, or about his timeworn insistence on running the fullback dive).[2]

It was his very ordinariness that elevated him into mythology. In person, he could be witty and charismatic, and he could also be imperious and unforgiving and outright ruthless, especially with the media, especially in his final years—but simply by enduring, he became a grandfatherly figure even to those who never knew him, in watching over the community, buffering it from the temptations of modernity, serving as a symbolic connection to a pastoral ideal about amateur sports that never really existed in the first place. And until November 2011, as Joe Paterno neared the end of his forty-sixth season as Penn State's head coach, the consensus was that the Grand Experiment, while imperfect, had been a rousing success.

And then, in a matter of days, everything went straight to hell.

IV.

"I have been doing a good deal of experimenting with the forward pass," Amos Alonzo Stagg wrote, "and I believe it is going to have quite an influence upon the game."

Stagg was by all accounts a brilliant tactician, experimenting with formations and shifts, opening up the game, freeing it from the mass-momentum plays that had bogged it down in danger

---

2. In his final years, they inevitably asked when he was going to retire.

and lethargy. While Knute Rockne and Notre Dame are often credited with advancing the possibilities of the pass, Stagg did it first: In 1906, the first year it was deemed legal, he created sixty-four pass plays. If Walter Camp was the father of football, declared *Collier's* magazine, then Stagg was its Thomas Edison. He won 90 percent of his games between 1906 and 1909 while playing in the Intercollegiate Conference of Faculty Representatives (which would later become known as the Big Ten), and when Stagg's Maroons went undefeated in 1913 (after 6-1 seasons in 1911 and 1912), one local newspaper called him "the greatest coach the game has ever produced."

Even as he was modernizing the game, he became a symbol, a source of nostalgia, author Robin Lester (in the book *Stagg's University*) wrote, for "a purer, less materialistic Christian America that had been lost." He had spent a year in divinity school at Yale; he reportedly coached one game while holding his baby son in his arms. In 1913, the University of Chicago named the football stadium after him.

Stagg was the most important and indispensable figure on campus, and he knew it. He was, wrote one newspaper, "the genius of the university advertising department," and he became so beloved by alumni that they could not imagine the school existing without him. He clashed with faculty, and he insisted upon autonomy for his program, and he promised that he would not interfere with academics but didn't always live up to his word. His team had its own residence hall, and its own training tables, and its own tutorial program. He and Harper, the university president, foreshadowed the concept of bowl games by embarking on a 6,200-mile, multigame barnstorming tour of the Pacific Coast in a private railcar provided by a woman referred to in the papers as a "kindly spinster."

In 1924, going up against Illinois's Red Grange, Stagg's Maroons managed a 21–21 tie and won the school's first Intercollegiate Conference championship. The football program brought in more than two hundred thousand dollars that season, and Stagg promised it would only get better. He was sixty-two years old, and he had no intention of stepping down anytime soon.

V.

My family moved to State College, the very season Penn State lost to Alabama on that goal-line stand in the Sugar Bowl. I was in first grade, and my social skills were stunted by an overpowering shyness, and so Penn State football became the language by which I could relate to the world and through which I could speak to the adults around me. I drew pictures of Curt Warner and D. J. Dozier; I memorized the rosters so that when people in our section at Beaver Stadium would ask, *Who made that play?* I could be the one to tell them. To this day, when I try to recall the combination of my gym locker or a friend's birthday or the license plate of my rental car, I think in terms of uniform numbers. It is not 31-17-03: It is Shane Conlan–Harry Hamilton–Chip LaBarca.

Those were great years, and Penn State was in its heyday, winning national championships in 1982 and 1986, going undefeated in 1994. One former player called it Camelot, and that sounds apt enough. Joe Paterno was named *Sports Illustrated*'s Sportsman of the Year in 1986; days after the issue went to press, Paterno's defensive coordinator, Jerry Sandusky, devised the brilliant game plan that allowed Penn State, in its austere two-tone uniforms, to defeat that flamboyant Miami team to win the national championship. That game was watched by more people than any other televised college football game in history. I still possess my original recording on a VHS tape.

I don't think it was an accident that Paterno's public profile peaked during the Reagan years (the Gipper gave a rambling and occasionally nonsensical interview at halftime of the Miami game), at a time when nostalgia served as political currency. Paterno, who campaigned for both Reagan and George H. W. Bush, fit the moment. He was a man straight out of a bygone era: He still wore those thick and unfashionable glasses, and he still rolled up his pants to keep the cuffs clean, and he still wore black athletic shoes with fat white tube socks. His likeness (the nose and the glasses) was omnipresent in State College—it got so that you stopped noticing it after a while—and yet he walked among us, too: I remember one Saturday morning in the autumn of my adolescence, the coach shambling along in his parka, brow furrowed, glasses shadowed in the sharp glare of the sun, black sneakers kicking at the leaves as they eddied and then parted on the asphalt path before him. I did not intend to follow him; it just happened that way, so that one moment I was headed to a football tailgate and the next moment I was trailing along behind Joe Paterno.

I spied on him for several miles that day. It was a routine of his to walk from his house to the stadium where he coached, slipping across campus, past science labs and classroom buildings and parking lots occupied by stunned tailgaters who could never quite get over the fact that it was really him. Sometimes we were guilty of regarding him as more deity than man, as if he presided over us in mythological stand-up form. He was as much our own conscience as he was a football coach, and we made that pact and imbued him with that sort of power because we believed he would wield it more responsibly than any of us ever could. Maybe that was naïve, but we came of age in a place known, in the vernacular, as Happy Valley, and I wonder now, when I think back on what happened, whether naïveté was part of the package.

VI.

The death knell of Chicago football began in the mid-1920s, and there was little that Amos Alonzo Stagg could do to stop it. The school's dean of the colleges circulated a memo that questioned whether the football program was living up to its ideals; a succession of university presidents did not feel the same regard for college football as did William Rainey Harper, and the school upped the entrance requirements for undergraduates under a program called the New Plan. The Maroons could not recruit with the same freedom as their local competitors. They lost spectators to Notre Dame and Northwestern and a fledgling professional team known as the Bears, and they lost spectators to the Great Depression. And they lost games, season after season, so much so that Stagg slowly bled away any political favor he may have gained. The appointment of his son to his coaching staff was reluctantly approved by trustees, one of whom said "it is precisely the thing that ought not to be done." In 1931, the *Daily Maroon,* the student newspaper, published an "Open Letter to the Old Man" that begged Stagg to depart before he was forced out.

Stagg had received an extension of service from the trustees when he turned sixty-five, and in 1933, at age seventy, he lobbied for another one. He was denied. Understanding he was nearing a point of no return, he'd written to the new university president, Robert Maynard Hutchins, a couple of years earlier. He asked to be named athletic director, to have near autonomy over the entire department, and to be permitted to coach football "for five years at least." And this was the turning point for Chicago, as an institution: Acceptance of Stagg's offer, Robin Lester wrote, "would also have constituted the most flagrant admission in America of the ultimate professionalization of the head coach."

Hutchins offered Stagg a choice of public relations jobs instead. Stagg declined. He was let go, and the football program never righted itself. In 1939, the Maroons opened with a 6–0 loss to Beloit, and then lost four straight games, to Harvard, Michigan, Virginia, and Ohio State, by a combined score of 254–0.[3] "It is a depraved system which has to depend on the prestige of eleven men to attract students to the university or to uphold the university's name," wrote the editor of the *Daily Maroon.*

It came down to a central question about the philosophy of higher education; it came down, Lester wrote, to the "elitist" versus the "egalitarian," and men like Stagg no longer held sway at

---

3. They did beat Oberlin 25–0, which probably explains why Oberlin doesn't have a major-football program anymore, either.

Chicago, which could now foresee a way to move forward as a university without bending to the inevitable compromises that the sport required. The school's president, Robert Hutchins, "became the best-known enemy of football since Charles Eliot [at Harvard]," wrote author John Sayle Watterson. He convinced an influential alumnus that football was now actively damaging the school's reputation, and together they convinced the board of trustees.

On December 21, 1939, the University of Chicago voted to disband its football program.

VII.

What was breathtaking about Penn State was just how *fast* everything seemed to turn: Over one weekend in November 2011 came a horrifyingly detailed indictment, centered around the revelation that Jerry Sandusky had been sexually molesting children for decades. And it was the cover-up, or at least the appearance of a cover-up, that made things even worse: Sandusky had apparently continued to prey on children—allegedly in the showers of Penn State's own football building—despite the apparent knowledge of a number of key university figures, including Joe Paterno. Either they were engaged in an active conspiracy to preserve the reputation of the program, or out of fear they had failed to act. Whichever it ultimately was, the results were inexcusable. A few days later came the dismissal of Penn State's president, and the ongoing indictments of the school's athletic director and vice president; before the week was even out, we witnessed the public firing of

Paterno on cable news, which took place on a Wednesday night and was followed by an aimless mob gathering downtown that resulted in the destruction of a television truck.

For years, we had concerned ourselves with how the Paterno era might end; he had always struck us as ageless until those final seasons, when the coach's fragility manifested itself all at once. During a game against Wisconsin in 2006, two players crashed into him on the sideline, breaking his leg. Before the 2011 season, he took a blindside hit during practice and wound up in the hospital. He sat in the press box during games, and his face began to droop, and he ceded much of the day-to-day control to his longtime assistants, and through nearly all of it he kept insisting, as he always had, that he could imagine doing this for at least five more years. The five-years line became a running gag through the 1990s and first decade of the 2000s; there was no more truth in it than there was in what much of Paterno said in his Tuesday press conferences, during which he could alternate between folksy and irascible in a matter of seconds.[4] We talked among ourselves, my college friends and I, about the worst-case scenarios, about whether he might come to his end right there on the sideline, or whether his career might explode in a flare of misplaced rage, as it had for Woody Hayes all those years before.

But this? The idea that Paterno could do something to uproot his entire legacy? No. This was almost as unfathomable as the crimes themselves.

---

4. "I don't know that much about what it is to be dead," he said at one particularly feisty media gathering in 2009. "How much do you know what's going on after you're dead?" As with pretty much everything Paterno said before the revelations of 2011, it now feels weirdly ironic.

*   *   *

Of course, the most terrifying lesson of Penn State is that patterns can occur that otherwise intelligent people either don't take the time to address, or refuse to notice.[5] From 2000 to 2004, for the first extended period in my lifetime, Penn State football fell into a deep and sharp decline, going 26-33 over the course of five seasons. A website was started specifically for the purpose of driving Paterno out; his players got into more legal trouble in and around campus than they ever had before. His son, Jay, hired as the quarterbacks coach, became a source of ire on message boards and in chat rooms. The program no longer seemed capable of competing at an elite level. According to a newspaper report, four Penn State administrators—including the president, Graham Spanier, and athletic director Tim Curley—came to Paterno's home at the end of a 4-7 season in 2004 and asked him to retire. Paterno refused. He told them, in so many words, to get the hell out of his house. A few months later, speaking at an off-season alumni gathering in Pittsburgh, he said, "If we don't win some games, I've got to get my rear end out of here. Simple as that."

I don't know if he ever really meant it. Maybe if Paterno had gone 2-10 the following season, he would have been forced into retire-

---

5. I really don't want to relitigate these crimes here, because I don't have any more answers than anyone else does, and I found that the factionalism and grandstanding that followed the Sandusky revelations—perhaps my own voice included—cheapened the revelations of the children who had been harmed. That said: I do believe Paterno deserved to be fired, simply because of what happened under his leadership. What I don't know—what I think we'll never know—is whether Paterno and the other Penn State administrators engaged in an active conspiracy to cover up Sandusky's actions, or whether they were simply too scared and/or oblivious. Either way, I suppose, the horror of the end result is the same.

ment, like Stagg once was. But Paterno did not go 2-10 in 2005; Paterno went 11-1 in 2005, and came a last-second loss to Michigan away from going undefeated. He regained his leverage. And the problem was that there was now no one who could tell Joe Paterno when to leave, or what to do, or how to handle the future of his program.

Would the Sandusky revelations have surfaced sooner if Paterno was no longer there? I don't know. I don't even know if it's fair to say Paterno was the most powerful man on campus, as so many people have speculated in the aftermath of the Sandusky trial—Spanier, like William Rainey Harper before him, imposed his philosophy on almost everything—but there is no question Paterno was the most *important* man on campus. Even if he was too old to be effective in his coaching job, he had an uncanny ability to raise money for the school's continual fund-raising campaigns; he'd earned such fealty among alumni that they simply couldn't imagine a Penn State without him.[6] Until they suddenly had no choice.

"I'm scared to death to retire, to be frank with you," Paterno had once confessed to a writer.

And two months after his firing, he was dead of lung cancer.

VIII.

In 1938, Amos Alonzo Stagg returned to the field that bore his name. He was in his mid-seventies, and he was coaching at

---

6. And that includes me. I wrote this for ESPN in 2009: "The reason I can't imagine such a thing is quite selfish: It's because if Joe Paterno goes away, I will have one more reason to face the fact that I am an adult."

the College of the Pacific in Stockton, California, and his team defeated Chicago, 32–0. By then, all that remained of the Stagg years was a sentimental yearning for what once was. "Regardless of its protests to the contrary," one alumnus wrote, "the University is becoming a school for intellectual geniuses and bookworms only."

Wrote another longtime campus observer: "Why is it that the Grand Old Man still holds such a grip on the affections of alumni? It is not, perhaps, because he is a symbol of our forgotten ideals, of our lost innocence?"

Amos Alonzo Stagg retired from his final job, as the kicking coach of a local junior college, at age ninety-six. He died in 1965, at age 105. In the 2013 *U.S. News & World Report* academic rankings, Stagg's University was fourth, behind Harvard, Yale, and Princeton, all of which burnished their reputations through major-college football and then made the choice to leave it behind.[7]

IX.

There is a place in my hometown known as Beaver Canyon, a stretch of downtown street bounded on both sides by towering student apartment buildings. In 1998, during an annual summer craft fair and alumni bacchanalia known as Arts Fest, someone hurled a garbage can off a balcony, and then someone else threw one of those party-ball kegs into the road, sparking a riot that pro-

---

7. The Ivy League schools now compete at the Football Championship Series level, one classification below "big-time." The University of Chicago now competes in Division III, which is nonscholarship NCAA football.

voked the spraying of tear gas and multiple arrests. In a way, what happened on that night in State College was much weirder than what happened the night Paterno was fired, because there was no explanation for it at all. But that riot didn't unfold on Twitter and Facebook and national television, with reporters from every major media outlet in America wandering our streets in search of conflict.

A couple of years before the scandal broke, NPR's *This American Life* aired an episode called "No. 1 Party School,"[8] and it was all about life at Penn State on a typical weekend, and it is sad and infuriating and yet weirdly uplifting in parts, when the alcohol poisoning and the fighting and the rioting falls away and you realize that we did the stupid things we did because we were kids and, at a school with nearly forty thousand undergraduates, we just wanted to forge some semblance of a community. Honestly, it's hard to know which came first anymore, the partying or the football, but for as long as I can remember, they've both existed in an undeniable symbiosis. And this is why the idea of college football remains so controversial, seven decades after Stagg's University opted for a new direction: It brings out the best of us and the worst of us at the same time.

After the mini-riot the night of Paterno's firing, I spent a lot of time explaining college football to people who didn't understand it. I found myself in conversation with people who had not grown up in circumstances like mine, who were raised in cities where the sports were largely practiced by professionals, and who had

---

8. Penn State was named the top party school in the country in a 2009 *Princeton Review* survey. I cannot say it was an undeserved distinction.

attended universities that had long ago chosen elitism over egalitarianism. And they asked me why the sport, with all of its dirty compromises, could possibly matter so much to the schools and the student bodies and the alumni bases that continue to pursue it with such fervor.[9] They asked me how college football could still matter to *me,* what with everything that had happened in my hometown.

And the answer I gave was both cynical and emotional. I told them that the reason why schools work so hard and often take ethical shortcuts to forge themselves into football powers was this: If they are successful, then the game serves as the lifelong bond between alums and townspeople and the university, thereby guaranteeing the institution's self-preservation through donations and season-ticket sales and infusions into the local economy. It is a crass calculus, when you put it that way. But also: Football ties the community together; football is such a powerful and meaningful force that it literally leads us into the streets to embrace each other.

And this is the one thing that Penn State has that Chicago never will again.

Is it worth it? It would be easy, given everything that's happened in my hometown, to say that it is not. And I suppose this is why there will always be critics and this is why there will always

---

9. On the same day in 1991 that thousands of Penn State students gathered around to pay tribute to a goalpost that was not the actual goalpost used in the football victory they were celebrating, a group held a protest of the impending Persian Gulf War on the steps of Old Main. Among us all, there was an underlying fear that the government might reinstitute the draft; we talked about it constantly that fall. "Knowing in your heart that something is wrong, but doing nothing to stop it," one student said, "is as bad as taking part, and maybe worse."

The protest drew a crowd of one hundred.

be those for whom college football is—other than our own families—the purest emotional attachment of our adulthood, and this is why there will always be those of us who bound between those two poles.

I mean, I *know* it's crazy, and I *know* it doesn't make rational sense. But there's a strange beauty about returning, every Saturday, to the places where we came of age: It allows us, as adults, to feel like true believers, even if that no longer means what we thought it did when we were young.

ACKNOWLEDGMENTS

It is common for authors, in acknowledgments such as these, to declare that their book would not exist without their editor; most of the time, this is meant metaphorically. But in this case, it is literally true. Brant Rumble (allegiance: *Auburn, and to a lesser extent Georgia Tech*) and I have been discussing the contents of this book, in its many potential forms, for more than a decade, mostly while watching college football games on varied couches in varied New York City apartments in varied states of sobriety. Only someone as exhaustively obsessive as Brant (I refer you to the footnote on page 162, or to his collection of Oasis EPs) could have championed this book—and refused to give up on it—over the course of all those years. (He's even undeterred by the fact that his wife is an Ohio State fan.) Daniel

Greenberg (*Wisconsin*) was there for both of us when the whole thing threatened to fall apart.

Thanks, also, to the other people on those varied couches who helped me flesh out these ideas, most notably Chuck Klosterman (*Notre Dame, Nebraska, North Dakota State, teams that wear orange as their primary color*) and Jon Dolan (*Minnesota*), but also Ben Heller and Brian Raftery (*N/A*), Sean Howe (*Empire State University*), Jim Cooke (*Syracuse*), Ryan Jones and Kevin Gorman and Damian Dobrosielski and B. J. Reyes (*Penn State*), Greg Milner (*Hawaii*), Bob Ethington (*Nebraska*), and Chris Ryan (*Miami, by ethos*).

Thanks to my editors at Grantland, especially Sean Fennessey, Dan Fierman, and Bill Simmons, for the opportunity; and thanks to my editors at Sports on Earth, Larry Burke, Steve Madden, and Matt Brown. Thanks also to my other favorite editor, Jay Lovinger.

Thanks to Theodore Goudge for the maps and the perspective.

Thanks to my mother and father, for choosing to move to a college town at an especially impressionistic moment in my life. And thanks to Cheryl Maday (*Northwestern*) for ceding space on our couch all those Saturdays, and for buying the couch in the first place, and for tolerating my often inexplicable college football compulsion (especially during fall weddings), and for not going to Michigan.

BIBLIOGRAPHY

In delving into college football's vast mythology, I relied on the work of dozens of authors who explored specialized aspects of the sport's history, including (most prominently) the ones below.

The American Football Trilogy: The Founding Documents of the Gridiron Game, by Walter Camp, Amos Alonzo Stagg, Lorin F. Deland, and Henry L. Williams.

America's Game: The Epic Story of How Pro Football Captured a Nation, by Michael MacCambridge.

Big Play: Barra on Football, by Allen Barra.

The Biggest Game of Them All: Notre Dame, Michigan State and the Fall of '66, by Mike Celizic.

Bowled Over: Big-Time College Football from the Sixties to the BCS Era, by Michael Oriard.

'Cane Mutiny: How the Miami Hurricanes Overturned the Football Establishment, by Bruce Feldman.

College Football, by John Sayle Watterson.

College Football and American Culture in the Cold War Era, by Kurt Edward Kemper.

The Fifty-Year Seduction: How Television Manipulated College Football, from the Birth of the Modern NCAA to the Creation of the BCS, by Keith Dunnavant.

A Fire to Win: The Life and Times of Woody Hayes, by John Lombardo.

Football Revolution: The Rise of the Spread Offense and How It Transformed College Football, by Bart Wright.

Hip: The History, by John Leland.

The History of American Football, by Allison Danzig.

Horns, Hogs, and Nixon Coming: Texas vs. Arkansas in Dixie's Last Stand, by Terry Frei.

King Football, by Michael Oriard.

The Last Coach: A Life of Paul "Bear" Bryant, by Allen Barra.

The Missing Ring: How Bear Bryant and the 1966 Alabama Crimson Tide Were Denied College Football's Most Elusive Prize, by Keith Dunnavant.

More Than Winning, by Tom Osborne with John E. Roberts.

No Ordinary Joe: The Biography of Joe Paterno, by Michael O'Brien.

Oh, How They Played the Game, by Allison Danzig.

Paterno: By the Book, by Joe Paterno with Bernard Asbell.

A Payroll to Meet: A Story of Greed, Corruption, and Football at SMU, by David Whitford.

Quotable Spurrier, by Gene Frenette.

Reading Football: How the Popular Press Created an American Spectacle, by Michael Oriard.

Rockne of Notre Dame: The Making of a Football Legend, by Ray Robinson.

Saturday's America, by Dan Jenkins.

Shake Down the Thunder: The Creation of Notre Dame Football, by Murray Sperber.

Stagg's University: The Rise, Decline, and Fall of Big-Time Football at Chicago, by Robin Lester.

Strange but True Football Stories, compiled by Zander Hollander.

Study Hall: College Football, Its Stats and Stories, by Bill Connelly.

Swing Your Sword: Leading the Charge in Football and Life, by Mike Leach.

Three and Out: Rich Rodriguez and the Michigan Wolverines in the Crucible of College Football, by John U. Bacon.

War as They Knew It: Woody Hayes, Bo Schembechler, and America in a Time of Unrest, by Michael Rosenberg.

Woody Hayes and the 100-Yard War, by Jerry Brondfield.

INDEX

8/14